BUILDING
THE
EMPIRE
STATE

Empire State Building from the south (postcard).

BUILDING THE EMPIRE STATE

Edited by Carol Willis

with essays by
Carol Willis and
Donald Friedman

W. W. NORTON & COMPANY
New York • London

in association with
THE SKYSCRAPER MUSEUM

Excerpts from Col. W. A. Starrett, *Skyscrapers and the Men Who Build Them* (1928), reprinted by permission of Simon & Schuster.

Excerpts from Paul Starrett, *Changing the Skyline* (1938), reprinted by permission of McGraw-Hill.

The text of this book is composed in Berthold Bodoni
with the display set in Broadway
Manufacturing by Quebecor
Book design by Charlotte Staub

Library of Congress Cataloging-in-Publication Data

Building the Empire State / edited by Carol Willis ; with essays by
Carol Willis and Donald Friedman.
    p. cm.
    Includes bibliographical references and index.
    ISBN 0-393-73030-1
    1. Empire State Building (New York, N.Y.) −Design and
construction−History. I. Willis, Carol.
TH4311.B85 1998   98-19117
690'.52'097471−dc21   CIP

W. W. Norton & Company, Inc.,
500 Fifth Avenue, New York NY 10010
http://www.wwnorton.com

W. W. Norton & Company Ltd.,
10 Coptic Street, London WC1A 1PU

0 2 4 6 8 9 7 5 3 1

To
Paul Starrett
William A. Starrett and
Andrew J. Eken

For the record.

CONTENTS

Preface

9

Building
the Empire State
by Carol Willis

11

"A Story A Day":
Engineering the Work
by Donald Friedman

33

Notes on Construction of
Empire State Building

47

Notes on *Notes*

185

Index

187

PREFACE

Reproduced here for the first time, *Notes on Construction of Empire State Building* was compiled in the offices of Starrett Bothers and Eken, the general contractor for the Empire State Building, probably in late 1930 and 1931. The notebook seems to have been intended simply as in-house project—even a labor of love—by someone, or several people, in the company. The document is not signed or attributed, and no one at HRH Construction, the successor firm of Starrett Bothers and Eken, knows who authored it. Indeed, it rested in storage at HRH for decades, known only to the few who had seen it. About ten years ago, I was lucky enough to learn of it and to make a photocopy. When in 1996 I tried to track it down again, I was unsuccessful until Lewis Weinfeld, an executive vice-president at HRH, made it available to me and to The Skyscraper Museum. It was displayed in our inaugural exhibition, *Downtown New York: The Architecture of Business/The Business of Buildings.* The Empire State, of course, is in midtown—yet the notebook is such a gem that it had to go into the show.

Notes is a unique document in several senses. First, it is apparently a single manuscript that was meticulously typed on blue-lined graph paper and collected in a simple three-ring binder. The seventy-seven pages of text (typed on one side of the sheet) are interspersed with black and white photographs ranging in size from 4.75 x 3.5 in. to 4.25 x 2.5 in. (12 x 9 cm./11 x 7 cm.) and mounted with black corners on thirty-two sheets of brown pressboard. These sheets carried one to four photographs, each identified by a negative number, date, and brief caption, typed on a white label edged in red. For this book, we have enlarged the photographs, placing them where they seem to best illustrate the text, and Donald Friedman has written longer captions that explain for the general reader the work or equipment featured. The rich color and hand-made, scrapbook character of the original document are evoked on the book's jacket.

Rare, and I think unique in its scope, is the detailed pictorial record of the building process presented in the notebook. Serial progress photographs commissioned by the builder have been a standard form of documenting the work of large construction projects since the late nineteenth century. The shots in the notebook, however, show not the progress of the structure, but the process of building, especially the equipment and materials of construction. The text likewise provides as complete an account of the organization of a work site as exists for any skyscraper.

Of course, the Empire State is not *any* skyscraper. The notebook is unique simply because of its subject. Extraordinary in 1931 for its exceptional height, sheer size, and unmatched speed of erection, the tower has since been exceeded only in height and mass. Its singularity persists in its majestic dominance of the midtown skyline.

The expertise in construction management of Starrett Brothers and Eken is continued by its successor firm HRH Construction, which remains rightfully proud of the firm's achievement in the Empire State. Large-scale commercial construction is a high-pressure business and a profession in which most of those involved are looking forward to finishing the current job, and getting on to the next. Not much of the history of the major companies has been kept or given to archives. Happily, the Empire State notebook and some additional records from the 1920s have been saved by HRH, and the museum is grateful to Lewis Weinfeld and Joel Silverman for making these available.

This book marks the first publishing effort of The Skyscraper Museum. I am grateful to Nancy Green of W. W. Norton, who had the interest to undertake this project and the energy to push it along. Part of the museum's stated mission is to search out and preserve important records of high-rise history and to present them to the public through exhibitions and publications within a broader narrative of tall buildings and their urban milieu. Our perspective extends beyond the more traditional definition of architectural records to include construction companies, engineers, building owners and managers, trade associations, the office as a work place, and the high rise as home.

The Skyscraper Museum is particularly indebted to Donald Friedman whose knowledge of historical building construction, clarity of writing, and good will have made this project possible. I thank Michael Gericke for creating just the right jacket. For their valuable service on this project, I also thank Michael Radice, Doug Bowmen, and, as always, Mark Willis.

Carol Willis,
Founder and Director, The Skyscraper Museum
New York City

BUILDING THE EMPIRE STATE

Carol Willis

The Empire State Building is New York's signature skyscraper. The tallest building in the world when it was completed in April 1931, the Empire State broke every record in the book. At 1,252 feet, it surpassed the Chrysler Building's quirky crown by 200 feet and the spire of the Manhattan Company Building at 40 Wall Street, third tallest in 1930, by more than 300 feet. Gargantuan in scale, it boasted 2.1 million square feet of rentable space, compared to the 850,000 square feet of the Chrysler Building or the 1.2 million square feet of the city's next-largest office edifice, downtown's behemoth of the pre–World War I era, the Equitable Building. The most astonishing statistic of the Empire State, though, was the extraordinary speed with which it was planned and constructed.

There are different ways to describe this feat. Six months after the setting of the first structural columns on April 7, 1930, the steel frame topped off on the eighty-sixth floor. The fully enclosed building, including the mooring mast that raised its height to the equivalent of 102 stories, was finished in eleven months, in March 1931. Most amazing, though, is the fact that within just twenty months—from the first signed contracts with the architects in September 1929 to opening-day ceremonies on May 1, 1931—the Empire State was designed, engineered, erected, and ready for tenants. Within this time, the architectural drawings and plans were prepared, the Victorian pile of the Waldorf-Astoria Hotel was demolished, the foundations and grillages were dug and set, the steel columns and beams, some 57,000 tons, were fabricated and milled to precise specifications, ten million common bricks were laid, more than 62,000 cubic yards of concrete were poured, 6,400 windows were set, and sixty-seven elevators were installed in seven miles of shafts.

At peak activity, 3,500 workers were employed on site, and the frame rose more than a story a day. No comparable structure has since matched that rate of ascent.

This incredible schedule could be kept for two key reasons: a team-design approach that involved the collaboration of the architects, owners, builders, and engineers in planning and problem-solving; and the organizational genius of the general contractors, Starrett Brothers and Eken. The role of the builders in both the design and construction process is the focus of this book, which for the first time reproduces a notebook compiled in-house in 1930–31 by Starrett Brothers and Eken. (For more on the notebook's uncertain authorship and other original documents, see the appendix, "Notes on *Notes*.") This essay is an analysis and appreciation of the builders' accomplishment, seen in the context of the history of high-rise construction of the 1920s. The following essay, by structural engineer Donald Friedman, likewise celebrates Starrett Brothers and Eken's intelligent organization of the job and explains how their methods pointed toward the development of fast-tracking and modern construction management that became the standard for large-scale projects after World War II.

Few historians have paid attention to the practices of the building industry or to the active role often played by the general contractor in the design process.[1] Both subjects deserve study, for as Andrew Eken noted, his company never took a job "unless we express ourselves in it from the very beginning."[2] The logistics of construction affect the options of the architects, particularly in commercial architecture where, literally, "time is money."

By far the most vivid and informative books on the building profession are three by leading figures in the industry from the 1920s and '30s. Two were written by the eponymous siblings of Starrett Brothers and Eken, Paul and William Starrett. They were two of the five Starrett brothers, all of whom worked in the industry, either in association or as competitors; four were builders, one was an architect. The youngest, William A. Starrett, published *Skyscrapers and the Men Who Build Them* (1928), perhaps the best book ever written on skyscraper development and construction. The men to whom he referred included all types—from financiers, architects, and engineers to ironworkers, day laborers, and, of course, builders. William (Bill) Starrett was a gifted writer, and one of the delights of his volume is the way he ranges between poetic passages and utterly rational analysis.

Seeming to identify with the skyscraper, he writes on the opening page: "I have seen the unfolding of practically the whole drama myself, for while I have just passed the half century in years, I have keen recollections of the building of the first skyscraper that could truly bear the name." Most of the book imparts technical information in language easily accessible to a general audience, in chapters on topics such as "Excavations, Shoring and Bracing," "Steel Erection and Derricks," and "Job Organization and Discipline." If this sounds like the prose might be dull, consider these passages:

> Building skyscrapers is the nearest peace-time equivalent of war. . . . The analogy to war is the strife against the elements. Foundations are planned away down in the earth alongside the towering skyscrapers already built. Water, quicksand, rock and slimy clays bar our path to bedrock. Traffic rumbles in the crowded highways high above us, and the subways, gas and water mains, electric conduits and delicate telephone and signal communications demand that they not be disturbed lest the nerve system of a great city be deranged.

He continued:

> The obtaining of materials near and far and the administration of all those thousands of operations that go to make up the whole are the major functions of the skyscraper builder. Knowledge of transportation and traffic must be brought to bear that the building may be built from trucks standing in the busy thoroughfares, for here is no ample storage space, but only a meager handful of material needing constant replenishment—hour to hour existence. Yet it all runs smoothly and on time in accordance with a carefully prepared schedule; the service of supply in peacetime warfare, the logistics of building, and these men are the soldiers of a great creative effort.[3]

The other two outstanding books about building, published in 1938 and 1937 respectively, are *Changing the Skyline* by Paul Starrett, the president of the company, and *The Towers of New York* by Louis J. Horowitz, who had earlier headed Thompson-Starrett, a competing firm founded by the oldest Starrett brother, Theodore, in 1899. Both are memoirs, authored with the help of professional writers, that offer colorful behind-the-scenes stories about people in the industry and about how they won or lost big jobs.[4] I quote from these now-rare books for their professional commentary and their flavor. In addition, I refer to numerous articles on various aspects of the construction of the Empire State published in professional journals in 1930–31, including a series of eleven articles in *Architectural Forum* written by the architects and engineers of the project. Such thoroughness of coverage on high-rise construction was unusual and reflected the deep fascination with the scale of the project, as well as the activity of the building's savvy public-relations department.

In "The Climax," the penultimate chapter of *Changing the Skyline*, Paul Starrett wrote,

> The story of the Empire State Building is truly an epitome of all that has preceded. In a few pages it tells all the spirit, the imaginative and technical daring, and even some of the frenzy, that animated the decade of which it was the culmination.[5]

By *climax* he meant both the capstone of his career and the high point of the building boom that had begun around 1923 and accelerated through the decade. During these years the total volume of office space in Manhattan nearly doubled, and more than fifty buildings of thirty-five or more stories were added to the skyline.[6] In midtown, especially near the transportation hub of Grand Central Terminal, these included the Chrysler, Chanin, Lincoln, and Daily News buildings, among many others. In the financial district, the Irving Trust Bank at 1 Wall Street, the Manhattan Company Building at 40 Wall, the City Bank Farmers Trust, and Cities Service Building were a few of the taller towers that redefined downtown's silhouette.

Cities grow in fits and starts known as real-estate cycles, and the tallest buildings typically come at the very end of a cycle. Mid-cycle in New York, around 1925–26, major high rises averaged between thirty and forty stories, but by the end of the decade, most new buildings were forty to forty-five stories, even on quite small sites. The greatest surge in construction came between 1929 and 1931. These three years saw, in addition to the Empire State, ten new spires of fifty or more stories, including the seventy-seven-story Chrysler Building, the seventy-story 40 Wall Street, and the sixty-seven-story Cities Service Building (also known as 60 Wall Street and 70 Pine Street) (Fig.1).

The major reasons for the increased number of projects and their greater height were escalating land prices and the easy availability of financing. When developers pay large sums for land, they have to pile more stories onto the lot in order to lower the proportion of the cost of the land per floor. The price of

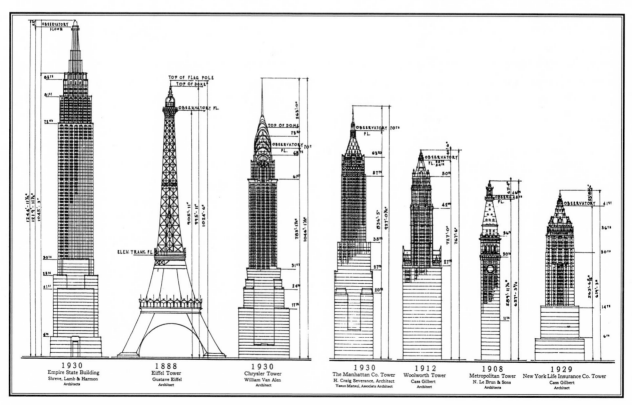

Fig. 1. Drawing from Fortune magazine, September 1930, comparing the Empire State to the Eiffel Tower, Chrysler Building, Manhattan Company Building (40 Wall Street), Woolworth Building, Metropolitan Life Tower, and New York Life Insurance Company Building.

land is a major factor in the complex real-estate equation known as *economic height*, which is the number of stories a developer must build to reap the maximum return on the money invested. Taller towers require more foundation, structural steel and wind-bracing, mechanical systems, and, particularly, more elevators and shafts. At some point for every skyscraper, rents for the extra stories do not justify the additional costs, and the owner will make more money by erecting a *shorter* building: that number of stories is the building's economic height.[7]

Although the Empire State is often described as 102 stories tall, the building is really an eighty-five-story, 1,050-foot-high building surmounted by an essentially ornamental tower. The so-called mooring mast for dirigibles rose an additional 200 feet, or the equivalent of seventeen stories (there are no real floors within the metal shaft). Of the office tower, eighty floors are served by the main banks of elevators, while for floors 81 through 85, and for the eighty-sixth-floor observation deck, visitors must transfer to a separate, short shaft of elevators. These top floors were originally used for offices of the developers and as service spaces. In other words, the Empire State was designed as an eighty-story office building: that was its economic height.

Securing the title of world's tallest building was clearly the aim of the Empire State's developers. Through the summer and fall of 1929, publicity had surrounded the construction of the Chrysler Building and the Manhattan Company Building at 40 Wall Street, which were vying for the record. In October, the Chrysler Building pulled a publicity coup when engineers hoisted into place the 185-foot steel needle that had been secretly assembled inside the "vertex," the pyramid that was the tower's distinctive crown. That move brought the midtown tower to 1,046 feet, surpassing the 927-foot Manhattan Company Building by more than 100 feet (and consigning it to relative historical anonymity). Early published drawings of the Empire State pictured a flat-topped eighty-story building, truncated slightly below the 1,000-foot mark. By November 1929, the owners and architects had added the extra five floors and conceived the 200-foot mooring mast that would clinch the record. (While there was obvious advertising value to holding the title, superlative height brought more than bragging rights: the observation deck reaped considerable revenue. During the first year, it brought in around $1 million—as much as the building earned in rents!)[8]

The Empire State was not just taller than all other skyscrapers, it was decisively *bigger* by almost every measure. Its net rentable area was 2.1 million square feet, as opposed to the 850,000 square feet of the Chrysler Building or 845,000 square feet of 40 Wall Street. The area of the tower floors was about 18,000 square feet, compared to about 7,900 and 8,100 for the other two buildings. There were sixty-four passenger elevators versus thirty-two and forty-one. The skeleton frame required 57,000 tons of steel compared to 21,000 tons for the Chrysler Building and 18,500 for 40 Wall Street. The drawing in *Fortune* in 1930 depicting the world's tallest structures gives a good sense of the Empire State's unprecedented size, even though it illustrates the building on its slender east-west axis, rather than from the broader north or south facades (Fig. 1).

The scale of the building makes all the more impressive its record for speed of construction. Erected in eleven months from the first steel columns to the finished building, the Empire State rose at the same rate as the Chrysler Building and 40 Wall Street—but it was twice the size. This record is less known and appreciated than the very visible fact of the building's great height.

Having reigned as the world's tallest building for forty years, the Empire State was eclipsed in the 1970s, first, by the twin towers of the World Trade Center in New York, then, by Chicago's Sears Tower. But even today its record speed of construction remains an unequalled achievement.

PAPER SPIRES

Why was the Empire State so big? The reasons were mostly economic—and perhaps partly hubristic. Conceived in the boom year of 1929, the building was a symptom of the speculative fever that drove up both the stock market and the heights of skyscrapers. The development strategy was to create an almost autonomous scale, "a city within a city" in the favorite phrase of the period. The building was designed to house 25,000, a floating population of some 40,000, and a maximum of 80,000. As one writer for *Fortune* observed, "It was a very spectacular gesture. If [the owners] were right they might . . . fix the center of the metropolis. If they were wrong they would have the hooting of the experts in their ears for the rest of their lives."[9]

The men who created the Empire State Building were not, in fact, real-estate "experts." The chief investors were Pierre S. du Pont, of the old-line family of Delaware industrialists, and John Jacob Raskob, a self-made millionaire who began his career as du Pont's personal secretary and rose through the corporate ranks to become a director of General Motors and one of the country's richest men. A number of their wealthy business associates were investors and served on the corporation's board of directors, but Raskob was the only one actively involved in planning the building.[10] The public face of the project belonged to former New York Governor Alfred E. Smith, who was signed on as the development corporation's $50,000 a year president, a position that was something of a gift from Raskob after Smith's crushing defeat in the 1928 presidential campaign (Raskob had been a financial backer of Smith and served as chairman of the Democratic National Committee).

Had these gentlemen been more seasoned in the world of real estate, they might not have had the nerve to place so large a building on the corner of Fifth Avenue and 34th Street. If, as the saying goes, the three most important factors in real estate are location, location, and location, then the Empire State had several disadvantages. It was was not in an office district, nor was it well served by rail or subway lines. Fifth Avenue between 23rd and 42nd Streets was principally a low-rise shopping district lined with fashionable stores that traded on a lively but leisurely street life. The tallest building in the immediate vicinity was the Internal Combustion Building, completed in 1928, which, though it occupied a full half-block, was truncated at twenty-eight stories.[11] While the Empire State's publicity noted that it was midway between the major train stations, and near several subways and elevated lines, the truth was that it was not *on* any.

We have gotten far ahead of the story, though, for the group led by Raskob did not assemble the land, but purchased it on the default of an earlier developer. It would be a mistake to think that they began the project with the intention of erecting the world's tallest building. Rather, the idea evolved, driven as much by economic calculations as by ego or ambition.

The typical pattern of Manhattan's transformation from low-density residences to intensive commercial use was grossly exaggerated in the history of the Empire State's site. Still farmland in the early nineteenth century, by the 1850s, elegant homes and spired churches graced this area of Fifth Avenue. On the west side of the avenue between 33rd and 34th streets stood the adjoining Astor mansions where New York's social elite, the Four Hundred, were lavishly entertained. By the 1870s, the character of the quarter was giving way to commercial uses, but the first significant violation of the residential scale was the thirteen-story Waldorf Hotel, built on the southern half of the Astors' block in 1893.[12] In 1897, the much taller Astoria Hotel was constructed, and the two buildings were joined to become the Waldorf-Astoria, world-famous center of elegance and epicurism. By the mid-1920s, though, many jazz-age New Yorkers considered the old Victorian pile a bit musty, and it began to suffer financially. Unable to resist the temptation of the skyrocketing value of their land, the owners announced that they would build a new, modern hotel on a full-block site uptown on Park Avenue.

In December 1928 the *Real Estate Record and Builder's Guide* reported the sale of the Waldorf-Astoria Hotel to the Bethlehem Engineering Corporation, Floyd Brown, President, and featured a nearly full-page rendering of a fifty-story building proposed for the site (Fig. 2).[13] The price of $14,000,000 (nearly $17,000,000 with additional expenses of leases, etc.) was the highest recorded that year. The drawing by the architectural firm of Shreve and Lamb showed a building with a massive base, multiple setbacks, and a rather stunted tower. It was described as a mixed-use stucture with nearly 2 million square feet of rentable space, with the lower twenty-five floors devoted to shops and lofts and the top twenty-five to offices.[14]

Brown, who was trained as an architect and had developed other large projects, may have intended to erect this building, or perhaps expected to sell his plans to another investor. A month earlier, he had paid $100,000 for an option on the property and contracted to pay $2,500,000 in two cash installments. He met the first payment, but defaulted on the second. On April 30, 1929, the day before the payment deadline, a syndicate was formed to buy out Brown's contract and develop the site; it was organized by Louis G. Kaufman, the president of the Chatham and Phenix National Bank and Trust from which Brown had borrowed $900,000 for the first payment on his contract.[15]

Such mid-deal changes in ownership were common in speculative construction, whether due to failures to secure financing or to opportunistic profit taking. A developer would locate a property suitable for a larger building and secure an option by putting up sufficient money to hold the lot for a year or by paying a deposit, so-called earnest money, on a contract of sale. He would then hire an architect to prepare an

Waldorf-Astoria Hotel in the Year's Largest Sale

Celebrated Hostelry Is to Be Replaced by Fifty-Story Office Building
Representing Investment of Approximately $25,000,000

THE sale of the Waldorf-Astoria Hotel last week to the Bethlehem Engineering Corporation. Floyd Brown, President, by the Bloomer-du Pont interests indicates the rise of realty values in the Fifth Avenue-Thirty-fourth Street district. The owners of the famous hostelry no longer could resist the tide of rising values, Mr. Bloomer in his announcement saying:

"While the Waldorf-Astoria still maintains its world-wide prestige and an unimpaired volume of business, the great non-producing areas of the hotel, involving enormous taxation and operating costs, have become so burdensome, a more profitable use of the site than for hotel purposes is indicated. This is the reason for the sale."

The transaction represents the largest and most important sale of the year. There have been numerous other large transactions during 1928, but none approaches the Waldorf-Astoria transaction in either amount of money involved, or in the magnitude of ground area. Nor does any other Manhattan project equal in ground area the proposed new building to be erected on the site, a fifty-story structure containing 2,000,000 square feet of rentable area and occupying 84,000 square feet.

While construction details of the new building are still being developed by Mr. Brown in association with the architects, Shreve & Lamb, and a number of managing and renting agents, the general plan as announced includes some unusual features. Chief among them are the vehicular ramps which will lead from Thirty-third and Thirty-fourth streets to a motor truck terminal in the basement of the building where trucks can be unloaded directly at the elevators. Another feature is a new street to be cut through the block between the building and the structure abutting on the west.

The new structure will occupy the 200-foot blockfront on Fifth Avenue and extend 425 feet west on Thirty-fourth and Thirty-third streets. It will be built in a series of setbacks for

(Continued on page 8)

Shreve & Lamb, Architects.

ARCHITECTS' SKETCH OF THE PROPOSED 50-STORY OFFICE BUILDING TO BE ERECTED ON SITE OF WALDORF-ASTORIA HOTEL

Fig. 2. Announcement of the sale of the Waldorf-Astoria Hotel and rendering of the proposed skyscraper in Real Estate Record and Builder's Guide, December 1928.

impressive rendering that was sent to the newspapers along with a press release. This publicity often attracted real-estate brokers who knew, or hoped to find, a major client interested in such a building. If a buyer appeared, the speculator could cash in for a quick profit. The potential for high returns, the small sum needed to initiate a deal, and the relative ease in securing financing for construction fired the burgeoning speculative market. Some sites changed hands four or more times before being built upon, making it possible, as William Starrett noted, "to turn a profit without turning a spadeful of earth."[16]

The new developers had much deeper pockets. In the summer of 1929, Kaufman proposed to du Pont and Raskob that they become the principal stockholders of the development corporation, which they did. At first, plans proceeded along the lines of Brown's original mixed-use project, but soon an important change of program was explored: transforming the building into a very tall "Class-A" office tower. In a letter of understanding written to Kaufman on August 28, 1929, Raskob confirmed his and du Pont's investment and attached a sheet of figures that compared the projected costs and income of two alternatives, a fifty-five-story and an eighty-story building.[17] The former was to contained 29,000,000 cubic feet, cost $45,000,000, and generate a rental income of $5,120,000, producing a gross return on total costs of 11.4 percent. The latter (the first building with another twenty-five stories piled above in a tower 80 by 240 feet) would add 330,000 square feet of rentable space, producing an overall income of $6,300,000, or a gross return of 12.6 percent.[18] The taller building was estimated to generate an additional $1 million in annual rents, which was a compelling argument for the risk of undertaking it.

In later years, associates described Raskob as the chief proponent of supreme height and recalled his boasts of planning "the biggest and highest building in the whole world."[19] At this early stage of the project, though, his tone was circumspect.[20] In the letter to Kaufman he wrote:

Our present tentative feeling is that we should be able to build a building, the cubicle content of which will be about 34,000,000 feet at $1.00 per cubic foot including all charges of every kind such as interest, cost of demolition, architect and builder's commission, fees paid for securing mortgages, rental fees, etc. etc. which would mean a total cost of not more that $34,000,000, which added to the land cost of $16,000,000 would give a total cost of $50,000,000.[21]

The figures in Raskob's letter of August 28 were based on standard real estate formulas, not on specific building plans. Indeed, from the acquisition of the property through the formation of Empire State, Inc. the plans for the building had been entirely financial, not architectural. The different schemes were described only in numbers—stories, cubic feet, operating costs, projected rents. No drawings were included or mentioned in these reports. Raskob's letter noted that one of the next steps would be choosing an architect to prepare a design.

On August 29, Al Smith announced to the press that the company would erect the world's tallest building on the site of the Waldorf-Astoria Hotel.[22] What had begun as a plan for a large, but anonymous mid-rise loft and office block was now transformed into an enterprise designed to capture the attention of the world.

In addition to the economic blueprint, there were a number of other conditions that shaped the building before architects designed it—in particular, the enormous size of the lot, the city's zoning regulations, and the rapid schedule of construction.

The Empire State could be as big as it was because its lot was about twice the size of most major midtown buildings. The assembled parcels of land of the Waldorf-Astoria Hotel and the Astor Court composed a site that was 197 feet long, the full block, on Fifth Avenue and extended 425 feet west on 33rd and 34th Streets (see photographs facing pages 4–9). A plot of this size, nearly two acres, was unusual in the commercial districts. Other than the blocks that later became Rockefeller Center (conceived in late 1929), the only comparable sites were the full-block lots on Madison Square occupied by the headquarters of the insurance companies New York Life and Metropolitan Life.

The size of the lot strongly influenced the design of skyscrapers after 1916, when the city's first zoning law set limits on the forms of commercial buildings.[23] Before zoning, buildings generally rose straight up from the lot lines for twenty, thirty, and even forty stories, making dark canyons of many streets. To protect some measure of light and air, the law introduced a new concept—the zoning envelope—into the vocabulary of urbanism. This was a formula (actually, five different formulas) that limited and defined the height and bulk of tall buildings by requiring that, after a maximum vertical height above the sidewalk (usually 125 or 150 feet), the building had to step

Fig. 3. Midtown skyscrapers near Grand Central Terminal, on a postcard, c. 1932. The setbacks required by the zoning law are visible, as well as towers of various dimensions, though none larger than 25 percent of the lot.

back as it rose in accordance with a diagonal drawn from the center of the street (Fig. 3). A tower of unlimited height was permitted over one-quarter of the site. This last condition had an important effect, for it made large sites particularly attractive for development because they allowed towers of profitable proportions. The Empire State's ample lot afforded a net tower area of around 20,000 square feet, which provided ample space for elevators and service rooms, as well as spacious, well-lighted offices. On sites that were considerably smaller, such as the 167- by 201-foot lot of the Chrysler Building, the tower floors either had less efficient elevator service or smaller offices.[24]

Another condition that affected the Empire State's design was the owners' requirement that the building be completed by May 1, 1931. This schedule was dictated by the real-estate practices of the 1920s, when leases were annual, commencing on May 1st. A building thus had to be completed by that date, or a year's rent revenue was lost. In addition, the running costs of interest and taxes for the Empire State were estimated to be $10,000 a day.[25] As a result, nearly every decision in the design and construction of the Empire State was affected by the need for speed.

These factors interacted and produced a complex equation that influenced the building's final form. The decision to erect the Empire State, how tall to make it, and what form it would take were worked out in figures on paper according to real estate rules, zoning formulas, and the requirements of finance before any consultants were hired to produce a design. As summarized in an article entitled "Paper Spires" in a 1930 issue of *Fortune*:

> These various elements fixed the perimeter of an oddly shaped geometric solid, bounded on one side by 83,860 square feet of land, on the other by $35,000,000, on the other by the law of diminishing returns, on another by the laws of physics and the characteristics of structural steel, and on another by the conical exigencies of the zoning ordinances, and on still another by May 1, 1931.[26]

A design with these disparate dimensions could not be planned by the architects alone. A team of experts—including the owners, builders, architects, structural and mechanical engineers, elevator consultants, and rental agents—was required to collaborate, first to define the problem, then to solve it.

TEAM DESIGN

The directors moved quickly to sign on their team. First hired were the architects, Shreve, Lamb and Harmon, who had developed the original loft and office-block proposal for Floyd Brown. The firm's chief business partner, Richmond H. Shreve, and

ROBERT H. SHREVE

WILLIAM F. LAMB

ARTHUR LOOMIS HARMON

Fig. 4. The architects: Richmond H. Shreve (his correct name), William F. Lamb, and Arthur Loomis Harmon. From Empire State: A History. New York, 1931.

William F. Lamb, the principal designer, had been joined in partnership in 1929 by Arthur Loomis Harmon. All were skyscraper veterans responsible for a number of the city's towers, including the New York headquarters for General Motors (Raskob's corporation) and 500 Fifth Avenue, Empire State's sixty-story sibling.[27] Theirs was a successful commercial firm accustomed to working with corporate clients and speculative developers.

Selecting the builder came next. Only a few general contractors had sufficient experience with this scale of operation and the capital necessary to cover the high costs of equipment and labor. In his autobiography Paul Starrett recounted that five major companies were interviewed. He did not name them, but besides Starrett Brothers and Eken, they were most likely the city's industry leaders in large-scale construction: George A. Fuller Company, Thompson-Starrett, Marc Eidlitz and Son, and Turner Construction.[28] In his interview, Starrett explained why his firm was the best-qualified builder, and cited the firm's recent successes, the skyscrapers for New York Life Insurance and the complex job at 40 Wall Street, which was just being completed in record time. He promised that Starrett Brothers and Eken would be able to demolish the Waldorf-Astoria and deliver a finished building in eighteen months and asked a flat fee of $600,000. Starrett Brothers and Eken was offered the job for $500,000 and accepted after some changes in the insurance and financing arrangements.[29] A letter of September 13 confirmed the agreement, and the contract was signed on September 20, 1929.[30] Demolition of the Waldorf began two days later.

From the outset, the owners, architects, and builder worked in committee to develop the building's program. This method avoided mistakes in design and costly delays in construction and to achieve significant economies through the design process. As Shreve explained, the complexity of large commercial buildings required skills beyond the traditional training of architects or any of the separate professions involved: "These problems must be dealt with through authority greater than the architect possesses" and would avoid "a duplication of effort and a loss of time too expensive to be tolerated in an operation requiring large capital investment."[31]

The success of the team-approach to design was universally praised by its members. Paul Starrett wrote:

I doubt that there was ever a more harmonious com-

bination than that which existed between owners, architects, and builder. We were in constant consultation with both of the others; all details of the building were gone over in advance and decided upon before incorporation in the plans.[32]

The group met regularly and worked closely with consultants on technical problems. These initial planning sessions occupied about four weeks in September 1929, and produced the complete technical, planning, and economic requirements for the project.[33] These guidelines became the basic program of the building. As William Lamb explained:

The program was short enough—a fixed budget, no space more than 28 feet from window to corridor, as many stories of such space as possible, an exterior of limestone, and completion date of May 1, 1931, which meant a year and six months from the beginning of the sketches.[34]

Within this basic program, the team searched for the most efficient and profitable design, developing several different versions of massing and height, each supported by cost estimates. Their seventeenth version, "Scheme K," was adopted at a meeting of the executive committee on October 3, 1929 (Fig. 5). While there were several subsequent changes, including the number of stories and the addition of the mooring mast, this scheme established the building's basic massing, plan, and proportions. In an article on the building's design, Lamb made a point of contrasting Scheme K with the previous version, reproducing the elevations and plans of both in order to show how the bulk of the base section had been reduced, light courts removed, and the tower made more integral.[35]

Key to the final design was the requirement that no office space be deeper than 28 feet, a real-estate standard. Through the first half of the century, sunlight was the principal means of illuminating the workplace and the most important factor in setting the dimensions and layout of the standard office. Rentability depended on large windows and high ceilings that allowed daylight to reach as deeply as possible into the interior. Ceilings were 10 to 12 feet in height, and windows were as big as possible without being too heavy to open, generally 4 to 5 feet wide and 6 to 8 feet high. As Lamb explained, these conditions affected the floor plans, as well as the building's overall form:

A certain amount of space in the center, arranged as compactly as possible, contains the vertical circula-

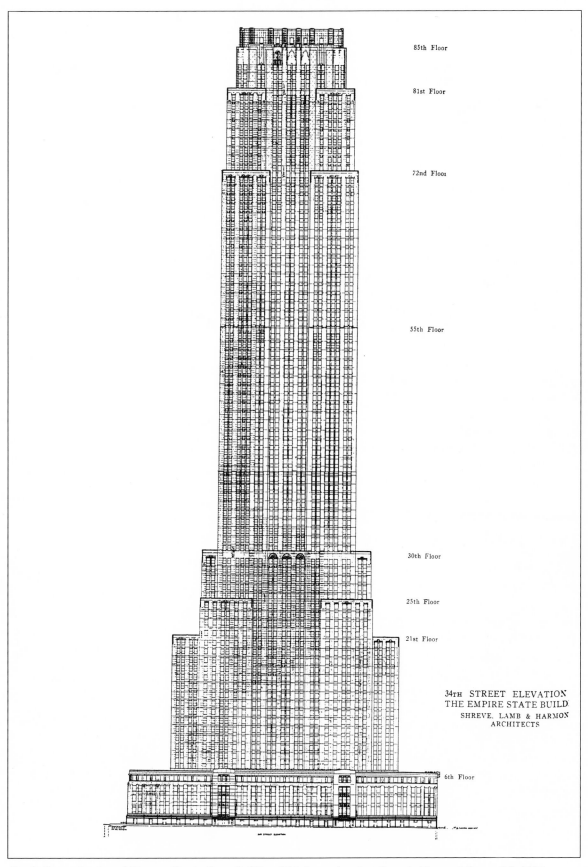

Fig. 5. Shreve, Lamb, and Harmon, Empire State Building, 34th Street elevation. From Architectural Forum, July 1930.

tion, toilets, shafts and corridors. Surrounding this is a perimeter of office space 28 feet deep. The sizes of the floors diminish as the elevators decrease in number. . . . The four groups of high-rise elevators are placed in the center of the building with the low-rise groups adjoining on the east and west sides so that, as these drop off, the building steps back from the long dimension of the property to approach the square form of the shaft, with the result that instead of being a tower set upon a series of diminishing setbacks prescribed by the zoning law, the building becomes all tower rising from a great five-story base.[36]

Thus, the massing of the Empire State was a direct expression of its floor plans (Fig. 6). The setbacks signaled the floors where the elevators terminated, while the height was limited by the core area needed for elevators. The precise location of the setbacks at the twenty-first, twenty-fifth, and thirtieth floors was also affected by the zoning law.

Interiors of skyscrapers are not constructed as separate offices, but as generic space that is subdivided and finished after a specific area is leased by a tenant. The full-floor plan is designed for easy division into an optimum number of individual offices. In the 1920s structural columns were most efficient when placed about 18 to 20 feet apart, which allowed two offices per bay.[37] These were generally 9 or 10 feet in width and had a working window. No office was rented without a window, because, in addition to admitting natural light, windows were used for ventilation. The dimensions of the single office cell and the spacing of the windows in large part determined the pattern of the façade.

The building's height was another issue determined through collaboration. As Paul Starrett recalled in his autobiography:

When the architects made their preliminary sketches, they found that eighty-five office floors reached about the height which could be constructed with the money available. Studies of elevator equipment showed that eighty-five stories also set about the limit of efficient and economical operation for elevators that could be installed in a building of this ground-floor area. In other words, the height, the beauty of the Empire State Building, rose out of strictly practical considerations.[38]

The process was more complicated, though. As noted earlier, the economic height of a skyscraper is a complex calculation that takes into consideration many factors. By far the greatest price of height lies in the requirements of efficient vertical circulation, for while elevators are expensive to build and to run, their major cost accrues in the unrentable space they consume for their shafts. The standard for a first-class office building is its elevator service, measured by the speed of the cars and, especially, by the maximum waiting time, which through the twentieth century has been 25 to 30 seconds. Because adding floors to a tower requires more elevators, space for offices on the floors below must be sacrificed.[39]

Architect Shreve and Bassett Jones of the mechanical engineers Meyer, Strong, and Jones explained in separate articles how the design of the building and the elevator system evolved through meetings with the owner, architects, builders, and engineers, and with the equipment manufacturers, Otis Elevator Company. Shreve wrote:

A program never before attempted was under discussion,—a larger elevator installation, greater car sizes, heavier loads, higher speeds and longer travel, than any previously known had to be set up, designed and made possible of installation in a relatively short time. Steel design, foundations, hatchways, clearances and electric service were involved, and the coordination of every agency participating was essential to success.[40]

Jones also emphasized the importance of the collaborative process from the earliest stages of design: "The proper simultaneous development of building, steel and elevator plans avoided the common error of attempting to fit an elevator plant into a previously fixed building arrangement and steel layout."[41] This meant that the space requirements of the elevator equipment were established before the structural drawings were begun.

Because of the large ground area and tower section of the Empire State and the proposed elevator system—single-deck high-speed cars in a hoistway, with all cars running to the street level—Jones concluded that the practical limit of the system was eighty floors. Even this height, he noted, could only be attained by using the largest practical cars traveling at the highest speed then available.[42] Together, the team decided that the best balance of efficient elevator service and well-lit office space meant reducing the base section of the building to five stories, above which the building set back considerably (60 feet). Jones explained:

Of recent tower buildings, the Empire State Building is unique in that the tower proper begins at the fifth floor, where a major setback occurs. At the fifth floor the yield area is about 69,000 square feet. At the sixth

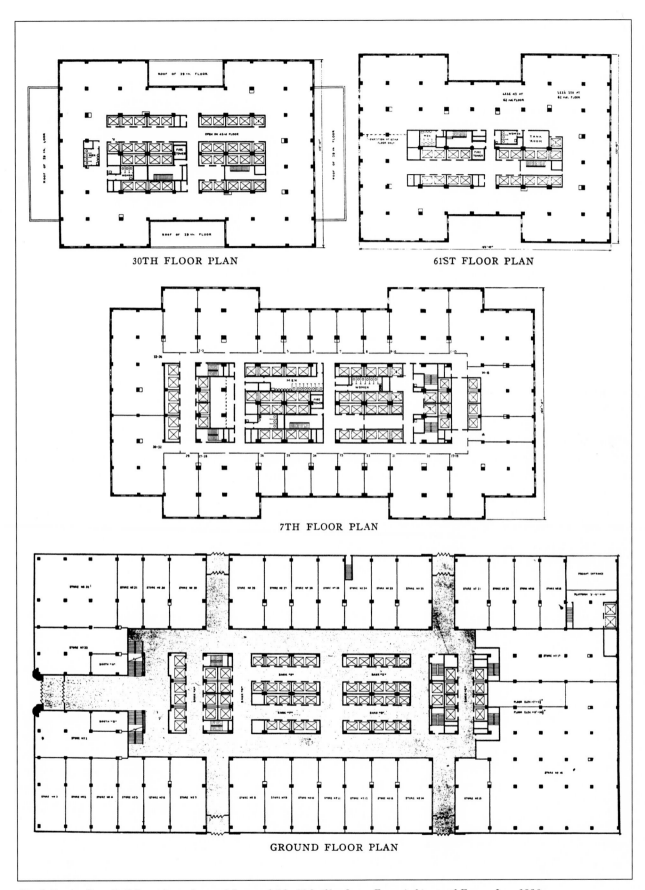

30TH FLOOR PLAN

61ST FLOOR PLAN

7TH FLOOR PLAN

GROUND FLOOR PLAN

Fig. 6. Empire State Building, plans of ground floor and 7th, 10th, 61st floors. From Architectural Forum, June 1930.

floor the yield area is about 30,000 square feet. In this way, ample light and air are obtained on all floors. This also has the result of reducing the number of floors having very large yield area to the five lowest, which, due to the short travel, makes it possible to serve these floors with a small bank of large elevators . . . Had it been decided to increase the number of large floors above the fifth floor, a condition would soon have been reached where double-decking would have provided the only practical solution.[43]

The requirements of the elevators thus affected the building's form in both its height and massing. Setting the height of the Empire State had little to do with engineering limits, and everything to do with economics. At the time, towers of 1,500 feet and higher were considered by most engineers to be structurally feasible, but while many articles discussed such soaring spires, no actual projects were initiated.

Throughout the design process, and especially in the critical months of September through November of 1929 when the major decisions about massing and height were made, team design and problem-solving by committee were standard procedure. The design of the façade and its window-spandrel-wall system evolved in similar fashion, as Shreve described in an article in *Architectural Forum*, "from the point of view of good sense, usefulness and economy,—and above all, the opportunity for most rapid erection." The aesthetic problem Shreve outlined was:

What treatment of these myriad openings in this vast expanse of wall would best retain and express solidity of mass, avoid giving the impression of a perforated shell, add dignity to utility, and through all escape the inherently monotonous gridiron of oft-repeated floors crossed by the slotted vertical bands of uniformly spaced windows?

His response did not directly engage the modernist debate around the role of the façade as an "honest" expression of structure, but identified with the issue: "Would not the mass of the building seem a more sturdy form if its outer shell or covering, for such only it is, were recognized and treated as a wrapping and not as a load-bearing structural element?"[44]

The solution was a system of stainless-steel mullions, limestone-faced piers, cast-aluminum spandrels, and double-hung metal windows. The design was in many respects innovative (as Donald Friedman explains in his essay). The aim was to standardize the elements as much as possible, creating a sort of kit of parts that would speed both fabrication and erection; for instance, in a total of 5,704 metal spandrels there were only eigh-

teen variations.[45] The specifications for some of these elements required new and specialized forms and were developed through close collaboration of the team and the manufacturer. For example, the design of the chrome-nickel steel used in the continuous mullions and the mooring mast, Shreve explained,

. . . involved the determination of the length and width of sheets which could be rolled and fabricated; the possibility of forming the sheet on the brake; the method of jointing and of bracing; the relation of the metal form to the exterior wall surfaces, the window heads, sills and jambs, and the spandrel; the means for attaching the metal form to the frame of the structure, as well as the finish and durability of the bright surface.[46]

Because the architects, builders, and subcontractors did not feel competent to develop the specifications on their own, they called in the subcontractors who rolled the material, representatives of the metal works fabricating it, those who were to erect it, and the inspectors who were to test the sheets at the several stages of preparation. Such a conference, Shreve noted, "made possible decisions based on instant comparison of recommendations and the establishment of the responsibilities of all those involved."[47]

This degree of attention could be sustained because of the scale of the Empire State. The size of any order for the great building gave the owners and their team leverage with the manufacturer or supplier. For this reason, and because the owners made the deadline of May 1, 1931 a part of the program, the Empire State could incorporate many features specifically designed to streamline the building process. As Paul Starrett claimed, in reflecting on his career, "Never before in the history of building had there been, and probably never again will there be an architectural design so magnificently adapted to speed in construction."[48]

THE BUILDERS' SHOW

There will be a neat and entirely legible sign on the board fence around the excavation reading George A. Fuller Co., Builders, or Thompson-Starrett Co., Inc., Builders, or Marc Eidlitz and Son, Inc., Builders, or Starrett Brothers and Eken, Inc., Builders. Below in equally neat but much less legible lettering will appear the architect's name. The difference in lettering expresses the relative importance of the architect and builder at this stage of the proceedings pretty

PAUL STARRETT

COL. W. A. STARRETT

A. J. EKEN

R. H. HUNTER

Fig. 7. The builders: Paul Starrett, William A. Starrett, Andrew J. Eken, and R. H. Hunter, a vice president of Starrett Brothers and Eken. From Empire State: A History. New York, 1931.

accurately. Between the completion of the plans and the opening of the doors, it is the builder's show.[49]

Of New York construction companies, Starrett Brothers and Eken were the premier skyscraper builders. Although the firm did not often rank among the "big five" in terms of total volume of new construction, by specializing in large-scale projects they were usually contenders for the big jobs. In 1930, the largest builder was George A. Fuller Company, with $29,099,000 in new business nationally. Marc Eidlitz and Son stood in second place, with a total of $28,612,000; James Stewart and Company was third, with $22,360,000. United Engineers and Construction and Todd and Brown, both with just over $16 million were fourth and fifth; Starrett Brothers and Eken was eighth, with $12,732,000.[50]

From 1927 through 1931, Starrett Brothers and Eken erected an impressive series of high rises that represented a range of challenges in construction of scale, speed, and complexity that few, if any, other builders could have met. These included the forty-story headquarters for New York Life Insurance (on a site only slightly smaller than that of the Empire State), the thirty-six-story McGraw-Hill Building on 42nd Street, a thirty-seven-story office building at 63 Wall Street, and the Manhattan Company Building at 40 Wall Street, which in both its height, seventy-stories, and its rapid construction, just eleven months, was a sort of rehearsal for the Empire State.

When they began the Empire State job, Paul Starrett had been in the building business for more than forty years, his brother Bill for more than thirty. Paul began his career in Chicago in 1888, working as a construction helper in the architectural office of Burnham and Root. These were boom years in the city's fortunes and the first exhilarating decade of the Chicago School's innovations in steel-frame construction. He stayed with the firm for six years, superintending many important jobs, including two pavilions for the 1893 Columbian Exposition. In 1897 he joined the George A. Fuller Company, supervising many large projects in major cities. A clear talent, Paul soon headed Fuller's New York office, serving as president for seventeen years.[51] Bill Starrett started in construction as a timekeeper for the Fuller Company. From 1901 to 1913 he worked at Thompson-Starrett, which was headed by his eldest brother, Theodore. During World War I, he organized the emergency construction section of the War Industries Board, erecting bases, hospitals, and flying fields with great speed.

(This was probably when he had the idea that "building skyscrapers is the nearest peacetime equivalent of war.") Returning to Fuller to work with Paul, he moved into an executive role.[52]

For different reasons, neither brother was at that time very happy with the direction of his career. Paul wrote in his autobiography:

> I had won as a builder success beyond my wildest youthful dreams. Yet, in a sense, I was a victim of my own success; for I was getting farther and farther away from brick and mortar and steel, the things I loved. As the head of a great corporation, with legions of lieutenants between me and the job, I merely passed on contracts and lunched with bankers and steel magnates. I imagine this often happens to men who fight their way upward and then, when they reach the top find themselves lost and unhappy—detached from the activities that satisfy them.[53]

Bill, on the other hand, had ideas about expanding the business into new areas, in particular, the design and construction of industrial structures. Impatient and ambitious, he was determined to form a new construction company, and he asked Paul to head it.

In 1922 the brothers launched their own company. They were immediately joined by Andrew J. Eken, a vice president at Fuller who had headed operations in Canada and for whom Paul had a warm personal regard.[54] The partnership became known as Starrett Brothers and Eken and in only a few years ranked among the giants of the industry. This achievement illustrates how the building profession depends on reputation and experienced management.

This said, what exactly does a general contractor do? The profession of general contractor developed in the late-nineteenth century as the scale of commercial building began to outgrow the traditional system in which owners or their architects contracted directly with the individual trades and suppliers, a method known as the divided contract. The single-bid, single-contract system was pioneered by George A. Fuller in Chicago in the 1890s to deal with the need to coordinate the increasing complexity and budgets of large-scale commercial construction. This method put a general contractor in charge of all operations. In *Skyscrapers and the Men Who Build Them*, Bill Starrett explained that under a general contract

> an owner turns over the plans and specifications for a building to a single agency, and that agency binds itself to deliver within a time limit a completed structure ready for the tenants to move in. The contractor finances the work from month to month, the owner,

however, paying the contractor a proportion of the actual outlay as the work progresses. The contractor buys and assembles the materials, lets the subcontracts himself, may himself perform certain of them, such as foundations, masonry, structural steel, and carpentry, supervises and administers the whole, and protects the owner against all contingencies, except the contingency of the owner himself changing his mind.[55]

In other words, management—of men, materials, and money—is the essential role of the general contractor. Bill Starrett also cited another definition he found apt:

Contrary to popular conception, the principal function of the general contractor is not to erect steel, brick, or concrete, but to provide a skillful, centralized management for coordinating the various trades, timing their installations and synchronizing their work according to a predetermined plan, a highly specialized function the success of which depends on the personal skill and direction of capable executives.[56]

Expert management was all the more important to Starrett Brothers and Eken because they always worked for a fixed fee, as opposed to the cost-plus basis favored by many other firms, including Fuller and Thompson-Starrett.[57] With a fixed fee, the builder had to estimate costs very accurately, because the expense of delays, unfilled orders, or other miscalculations came out of the company's profits; conversely, any savings became its gain. For the Empire State, Paul Starrett's bid of $600,000 (and the negotiated fee of $500,000) was based on little more information than the owners' figure of 34 million cubic feet. His long experience in the industry and his expert knowledge of building costs allowed him to commit to a fee before there were any architects' drawings or specifications.

More detailed cost estimates were prepared in the so-called buyout phase, which involved hiring the subcontractors. Normally, this phase consumed about six weeks or more when subcontractors consulted the plans and prepared bids. As Bill Starrett, explained:

These [subcontracted] items compose about eighty per cent of the cost of the building and include subcontracts such as steel, elevators, plumbing, electrical, heating, ventilating, plastering, painting and decorating. Another ten percent goes for commodity materials such as sand, cement, brick and similar items. Assuming the plans and specifications to be very accurate and complete, among any group of four or five competent builders, the bids on this ninety per

cent of the work will be nearly identical, unless some of them gamble on their profit by selling short on futures. The remaining ten per cent of the building cost is the builder's direct payroll, which usually includes the foundations, masonry, bricklaying, carpentry, etc. He might perform the fraction carelessly and make it cost a little more, or he might perform it so skillfully as to cut the cost of this direct payroll work as much as ten per cent. The difference either way would be only one per cent of the whole cost.[58]

Estimating and tracking costs, organizing the work site, and keeping on schedule were of the greatest importance throughout the building process. The first part of the *Notes*, from pages 9 to 20, focuses on these management issues. The section entitled "Job Organization" (also known as field organization) begins with a diagram of the various departments that shows forty-four jobs or areas and more than eighty individuals (page 9). Under the Job Superintendent, J. W. Bowser, were managers of departments, the most important of which were: the Job Runner, Construction, Accounting (which included Timekeeping and Payroll), and Cost and Production. The text outlines the functions of these divisions and offers intriguing glimpses into the builder's methods of supervision. One example is the field time-checking system, which involved daily hiring, laying off, and checking the workers on site (page 11). This was accomplished with a hiring ticket, a numbered brass check, and a staff of checkers who made rounds four times a day to verify the worker's presence. The number of hours each individual worked that day was then forwarded to the payroll division where it was posted and audited. At the end of the payroll week, empty envelopes bearing the workers' names and numbers were sent to the armored service, to be filled at the bank and brought back to the site for distribution on payday.

Another example of meticulous supervision was the calculation of daily labor unit cost. This was explained in the *Notes* and also at greater length in an article published in April 1931 in *Architectural Forum*, by John P. Carmody, the Assistant to the Superintentent in the division of Production and Cost Distribution.[59] (This piece so closely parallels the text of the notebook that Carmody may have been the author of at least that section of the notebook—or another writer prepared both versions.) Carmody wrote:

Entirely independent of the field time checking force is a field labor cost distribution organization, which checks each man in the field in relation to the kind of work he is doing. A summary is made for each trade or class on the foremen's daily reports, which show on one side the number of men and the total hours each man worked for the day and on the other side, the distribution of activities under the different accounting sub-division symbols. This insures, as far as possible, an accurate record of the work performed by each man every day. A digest of the activities is incorporated in the daily job diary, which gives a complete record of the day's activities.

In addition, a survey is made each day of the various quantities put in place of all those accounts upon which a daily cost unit is worked out. Once a week, a physical inventory is taken of the different kinds of material on hand, which serves as a check against quantities surveyed in place in the structure. The division of the various quantities placed, by the cost of labor, results in the daily cost unit.[60]

Some of these calculations can be seen in the "Analysis of Cost" appendix to the *Notes*.

A sample of the daily job diary followed the section on field organization. The daily construction report for August 14, 1930 went on for seven pages. As was standard practice, it logged every worker by trade or by subcontractor and described the work assigned for that day. There were 1,928 persons employed directly by Starrett Brothers and Eken and 1,511 by the subcontractors, for a total of 3,439 people. The lists are among the most amazing pages of the *Notes*; together with the many photographs of nameless workers, they record the human effort of the great enterprise.

After a long section on plant and equipment including elevators and hoists, the *Notes* turned to the distribution of materials, which presented two major aspects: scheduling of deliveries and moving materials efficiently in both vertical and horizontal directions. Paul Starrett wrote that given the careful planning of the design team: "Our job was that of repetition—the purchase, preparation, transport to the site, and placing of the same materials in the same relationship, over and over. It was, as Shreve the architect said, like an assembly line—the assembly line of standard parts."[61] The main challenge was to keep the line moving with a continuous feed of materials to the men, whose numbers could always be increased. To keep pace, materials had to arrive at the site on a precise schedule. This was true not only for the structural steel, which had to be placed at the specific point for which it had been engineered and milled, but also for mass materials, such as the ten million common bricks and the 198,000 cubic feet of limestone used

in the building. Since there was no storage room for these supplies, the goal was to move the materials only once—from the truck on which they arrived to the floor where they would be used, generally within three days. Eken called the Empire State essentially "a vast scheduling job" and claimed: "We ran trucks for that one the way they run trains in and out of Grand Central. If a truck missed its place in line on Tuesday, it had to wait until Wednesday to get back in."[62] The ground floor of the building was kept free of temporary structures so that trucks could drive in to deliver their materials. The *Notes* recorded that at peak operations about 500 trucks a day unloaded inside the building. That was nearly one truck every minute of the eight-hour work day—and that does not count the structural steel hoisted by outside derricks.

As evidenced by the extended discussion in the *Notes* the builders were particularly proud of several innovations in the materials delivery system developed for the Empire State. These included the overhead trolley, the narrow-gauge industrial railway, and the brick dump cars. Paul Starrett described some features of the system:

We handled and distributed all material by industrial cars on narrow-gauge tracks, running completely around the perimeter of the building on each floor, with the tracks extending across the platform of the hoist, so that cars loaded, for instance, in the basement, could readily run on the hoist and off at the proper floor and deliver at almost the spot where the material was to be used. Brick arriving at the job on the first-floor level was dumped into large bins in the first basement. These bins, with inclined bottoms, allowed the brick to slide through doors and drop into industrial dump cars after being thoroughly wet down. The cars deposited the brick alongside the layers, without having been handled from the time they came into the building until the bricklayer placed them in the wall. Under the old method of wheelbarrows, we could hoist only two barrows containing 100 brick per trip on a standard platform. With the industrial car and the same hoist, we carried 400 brick per trip. [63]

During the summer of 1930, construction hummed with over 3,400 men on site daily. There were established standards for efficient construction: for steel, three and a half stories per week; for brick walls, a story a day; and for stonework, one to two stories a week. In 1929 Starrett Brothers and Eken maintained this pace erecting the Manhattan Company Building at 40 Wall Street. But as Paul Starrett explained in his autobiography: "It was clear to us at once that on the Empire State we could never finish the building on time by any such progress. We decided to discard all these plans of operation and determined to erect the Empire State at the rate of a story a day."[64]

The last major section of the notebook is subtitled "The Fascination of Speed" and concentrates on the four pacemakers of the construction: structural steel erection, concrete floor arch construction, exterior metal trim and aluminum spandrels, and exterior limestone (pages 40ff). Starrett Brothers and Eken were extremely proud of the innovations they developed in these four areas, which are described in detail in the notebook. Donald Friedman expands on these explanations in his essay, clarifying for the non-builder both the complexity of the problems and the cleverness of Starrett Brothers and Eken's solutions.

In his autobiography, Paul Starrett called attention to two particular innovations that allowed the efficient movement of materials. In addition to the narrow-gauge industrial rail, he described the system for hoisting the limestone:

> For the setting of our stonework, we cut out altogether the customary derrick. The stone trucks drove into the building with the stone in crates, which we call skips or slings. Marked for its proper section of the building, each crate was lifted off the truck by a small crane, operating from a monorail on the ceiling, and delivered to the flatcars of the industrial railway. Taken to the proper floor, it was unloaded at almost the exact location in which it was to be set. Two hoists handled all the stone for the building, not only eliminating a large number of hoisting derricks and engines but, since the hoisting was inside the building, doing away with a grave source of danger to the public.

As a result, Starrett boasted:

> "We not only beat the stone-setting schedule by fourteen days, but for one period of ten consecutive days averaged 1.4 stories a day.[65]

Other records were set. The notebook records that for the structural steel, the time gained was twelve days. The concrete floors were finished four days ahead of schedule. The exterior metal trim and cast-aluminum spandrels were completely erected on October 17, 1930, thirty-five days ahead of their December 1 schedule. The time gained for the exterior limestone and its brick backing was seventeen days (page 41). "On time and on budget" is the phrase that warms the heart of developers and their

general contractors. With the systems designed by the builders and the concerted collaborations of the architects and engineers, and manufacturers, Paul Starrett noted, "We built the Empire State building for something like $2,000,000 under the original estimate."[66] The final cost of the building was $25 million.[67]

Not everything went so smoothly. While they were erecting the Empire State, Starrett Brothers and Eken were the contractors for two large projects in Newark and Cincinnati that were closed down for six weeks by the ironworkers' union. The Empire State was not struck, even though its steel erectors Post and McCord did employ nonunion ironworkers. Still, the effects of the bitter dipute and the financial losses on the Carew Tower complex in Cincinnati, in which the Starrett Brothers Corporation had a financial interest, were a strain.[68] "The Climax" chapter of Paul Starrett's autobiography ends not with bravado for his achievement, but with the startling statement:

> After forty years of intense activity, the strain of erecting the Empire State Building in eleven months was too much for me and I suffered a rather severe nervous breakdown.[69]

MAY 1, 1931–AND AFTER

Opening day ceremonies went off as planned with ribbon-cutting, dignitaries, and radio broadcasts. As president of the Empire State Corporation, Al Smith was center stage to receive most of the credit, and he bantered with the assembled politicians, including Governor Franklin D. Roosevelt and Mayor James J. (Jimmy) Walker, who all made speeches. Paul Starrett also spoke at the formal luncheon on the eighty-sixth floor ("the world's loftiest meal"), as did Shreve, representing the architects.[70] There was an RKO radio broadcast and formal party that evening, and the public was invited to visit the building the following day.

But for all the well-deserved congratulations on the building's quality and construction, the Empire State was shaping up to be a colossal financial failure. Three key factors contributed to its problems: the city's oversupply of new office space in the early 1930s, the Depression economy, and the building's problematic location. In the twenties New York experienced two surges of construction and brief scares about overbuilding, but demand kept up with the expanding supply until the stock market crash in late October 1929.[71] Even after Black Thursday, many projects proceeded because contracts were already signed and money committed, and because well into 1930, many in the real estate industry maintained that the economic downturn would be only temporary.[72]

The poor economy soon began to have an effect on renting, and when the bulge of new construction initiated in 1929 came onto the market, the vacancy rate rose, reaching nearly 25 percent in 1934.[73] New buildings were hit especially hard because many companies could no longer afford to move, and landlords in older buildings often offered discounts to retain tenants. Rates for the Empire State were set well below those of the denser business districts: on average they were 30 percent lower than first-class buildings around Grand Central Terminal and 40 percent below the financial district.[74] Nevertheless, in 1933 only one quarter of the space in the Empire State had been rented; fifty-six floors were completely empty, left as raw space. Not until the end of the 1940s was the building fully occupied and in the black.[75]

The hard times that hit all real estate investments were magnified by the size of the great empty tower. Why was the Empire State particularly slow to rent? The building's distance from the major office districts may have reduced its appeal. From the mid-1930s,

there was serious competition from Rockefeller Center, a three-block complex in a pioneering location that was somewhat closer to Grand Central and in the direction of the northward expansion of the business and retail districts on Fifth and Madison Avenues and, after World War II, on Park Avenue.

Yet the relative remoteness of the Empire State has been one of the reasons for its enduring power as an icon. While most New York towers cluster in nodes of business, the Empire State stands gloriously alone. Its majestic silhouette can be seen from all over the city and from distant approaches, as if fixing a center axis of Manhattan.

The story of the Empire State told in *Notes* is an understated drama. Its stunning statistics are generally delivered in a matter-of-fact style that often disguises the proportions of the achievement. Occasional flourishes strive to give import to the account, and the last page of the notebook is replete with passages from Ruskin and musings on posterity. But one simple sentence truly impresses:

Within a period of twenty-one months, the entire project was conceived and brought to a successful conclusion.[76]

That was the builders' show.

NOTES

1. Some who have include Paul Louis Bentel, "Modernism and Professionalism in American Architecture, 1919–1933," (Ph.D. diss., Massachusetts Institute of Technology, 1993); and Robert Bruegmann, *Architects and the City*: Holabird and Roche of Chicago, 1880–1918 (Chicago: University of Chicago, 1997), especially on George A. Fuller, 82.

2. Anon., "The Skyline Builders," *Fortune* (1950): 95.

3. Col. W. (William) A. Starrett, *Skyscrapers and the Men Who Build Them* (New York: Charles Scribner's Sons, 1928), quotations, 1, 63, 66; he discusses his brothers, 6–12. He considered the first skyscraper to be the Home Insurance Building in Chicago (1883–1884), designed by William LeBaron Jenney.

4. Paul Starrett, *Changing the Skyline: An Autobiography* (New York: McGraw-Hill, 1938). According to his grandson, Paul Pierson, the book was ghost written with Philip Freund. Also see Louis J. Horowitz and Boyden Sparkes, *The Towers of New York: The Memoirs of a Master Builder* (New York: Simon and Schuster, 1937).

5. P. Starrett, 284.

6. The number of tall buildings is my count, based on lists in W. Parker Chase, *New York: The Wonder City, 1932* (New York: New York Bound, 1983). For a discussion of the real-estate cycle in New York in the 1920s, building heights, and total volume of space in the business districts, see Carol Willis, *Form Follows Finance: Skyscrapers and Skylines in New York and Chicago* (New York: Princeton Architectural Press, 1995), 45–46, 166–168.

7. For a period explanation of economic height see W. C. Clark and J. L. Kingston, *The Skyscraper: A Study in the Economic Height of Modern Office Buildings* (New York: American Institute of Steel Construction, 1930); also see Willis, *Form Follows Finance*, 45–46, 166–168.

8. The building's total income for rents and admissions to the observation deck for the first year was $2,016,980, of which rents were $1,015,893.62, according to various files in the du Pont Papers at the Hagley Museum and Library, Longwood Mss., 229-15, Box 2, Empire State, Inc., 1932.

9. Anon., "Paper Spires," Fortune (September 1930): 58.

10. The Empire State, Inc. was officially incorporated on September 5, 1929. The directors of the Corporation were Pierre S. du Pont, John J. Raskob, Louis G. Kaufman, and Alfred E. Smith, along with Ellis P. Earle, August Heckscher, and Michael Friedsam. Copies of the documents of incorporation are in the du Pont Papers at Hagley Museum and Library, Longwood Mss., 229-25,

Box 5, bound volume, Empire State Inc. I discuss the background of the developers' decision making in greater detail in my article, "Form Follows Finance: The Empire State Building" in *The Landscape of Modernity: Essays of New York City, 1900–1940*, Eds. David Ward and Olivier Zunz (New York: Russell Sage, 1992), 160–190.

11. Chase, 215.

12. M. Christine Boyer, *Manhattan Manners: Architecture and Style, 1850–1900* (New York: Rizzoli, 1985), 32, 48–50, 227; and Robert A. M. Stern, Gregory Gilmartin, and John Massengale, *New York 1900* (New York: Rizzoli, 1983), 254–261.

13. Anon., "Waldorf-Astoria Hotel in the Year's Largest Sale: Celebrated Hostelry Is to Be Replaced by Fifty-Story Office Building Representing Investment of Approximately $25,000,000," Real Estate Record and Guide, 122 (29 December 1928): 7–8.

14. Several sources called the project an office building, but William F. Lamb described this first design as a "loft-type" building in his article, "The Empire State Building: The General Design," *Architectural Forum* 54 (January 1931): 7. Paul Starrett also described Brown's scheme as a loft building in Changing the Skyline, 285.

15. The precise nature of Brown's deal and what happened to him afterward is not entirely clear; his name does not appear in any subsequent list of investors. These financial dealings are detailed in my article, "Form Follows Finance," 165–169.

16. W. Starrett, 110.

17. Letter sent by Raskob to Kaufman, 28 August 1929, Hagley Museum and Library, Longwood Mss., 229-15, Box 1, file 26, I.

18. The figures used in estimating the rental rate ($3.25 per square foot and $4.00 for the tower) and operating costs ($.75 per square foot) were both for office space. The estimated construction costs were the same for both buildings, even though tall buildings were more expensive to build; one might therefore suspect that the person who devised the comparison wanted to tilt the figures toward the taller building.

19. From the limited correspondence that exists for this period (May to September 1929) it does seem that Raskob was the leader in the drive for record-breaking height, but there is no document among his papers at Hagley Library that states this directly. Associates such as Hamilton Weber, the rental agent for the building, later credited him with the idea; see Theodore James Jr., *The Empire State Building* (New York: Harper and Row, 1975), 45.

20. The only reference to the scale of the project came in Raskob's remark at the end of the letter: "I appreciate the opportunity you have given us in this matter and particularly in the privilege of being associated with you and your group in the doing of something big and really worth while. I am sure it will be the most outstanding thing in New York and a credit to the city and state as well as to those associated with it." In the context of the entire letter, Raskob's comment seems to me to express optimism, but hardly a hubristic compulsion to erect the world's tallest tower. Letter from Raskob to Kaufman, 28 August 1929, op. cit.

21. Ibid.

22. Empire State, Inc. was officially incorporated on September 5, 1929. See "Smith to Help Build Highest Skyscraper," *The New York Times* (30 August 1929): 1.4.

23. For a fuller discussion of the effects of the 1916 zoning law on the forms of tall buildings, see Willis, *Form Follows Finance*, 67–79.

24. For example, the tower floors of the Chrysler Building contained only about 7,600 net floor space; for plans and further discussion, see *Form Follows Finance*, 82–85.

25. "Paper Spires," 119, 122. The article also noted that the carrying charges on the two mortgages were estimated at $2,132,500.

26. "Paper Spires," 119.

27. Before establishing their own practice in 1924, Shreve and Lamb had worked in the office of Carrere and Hastings, where they had designed major New York buildings such as the Standard Oil and Fisk buildings. Harmon had worked independently until 1929; his best-known building was the Shelton Hotel (1924).

28. Paul Starrett described his interview for the Empire State commission in *Changing the Skyline*, 289–292. Another possible candidate was Fred T. Ley and Company, who erected the Chrysler Building.

29. Ibid.

30. "Paper Spires," 119.

31. R. H. Shreve, "The Empire State Building Organization," Architectural Forum 52 (1930): 770–774.

32. P. Starrett, 293.

33. The collaboration was by all reports exemplary; Paul Starrett, Shreve, and Lamb praised the team in Lamb, "General Design," 1, 5. Also see the comments of Shreve in "Building Organization," 771–774.

34. Lamb, 1.

35. Lamb, 1–4.

36. Lamb, 5.

37. Arthur Loomis Harmon, "The Design of Office Buildings," *Architectural Forum* 52 (June 1930): 819.

38. P. Starrett, 296.

39. Efficiency was measured in the number and speed of elevators, and related to travel time, and especially waiting time. Albert Kahn, "Designing Modern Office Buildings," *Architectural Forum* 52 (June 1930): 776.

40. Shreve, "Building Organization," 774.

41. Bassett Jones, "The Empire State Building. VIII. Elevators," *Architectural Forum* 54 (January 1931): 98.

42. Jones, 97.

43. Jones, 98–99. The Empire State was the largest contract ever let for a single building. The entire system cost around $4 million. The total length of the hoistways was

nearly 7 miles, and the one-way traffic capacity was 30,000 persons an hour.

44. Shreve,"Building Organization," 774.

45. H. R. Dowswell, "The Empire State Building XI. Materials of Construction," *Architectural Forum* 54 (May 1931): 625.

46. Shreve, "Building Organization," 774.

47. Ibid.

48. P. Starrett, 296.

49. Anon., "Skyscrapers: Builders and Their Tools," *Fortune* (October 1930): 85.

50. "Big 5 Retains Building Lead Through 1930," *(Washington D.C.) Herald* (22 March 1931), from a clipping from Empire State Building scrapbooks, Special Collections, Avery Architectural and Fine Arts Library, Columbia University.

51. For biographical information on Paul Starrett, in addition to *Changing the Skyline*, see Horowitz, *The Towers of New York*, 67–71, 104–106, and *Dictionary of American Biography*, Vol. 26, Supplement 6 (1956–1960), 592–593.

52. For biographical information on William Starrett, in addition to *Skyscrapers and the Men Who Build Them* and *Changing the Skyline*, see *Dictionary of American Biography*, Vol. 17 (1953), 536–537.

53. P. Starrett, 257.

54. P. Starrett, 206–208, 260. After Paul Starrett retired in 1938, Eken became president of the company (William Starrett died in 1932).

55. W. Starrett, 87.

56. This definition of the role of the general contractor was offered by engineer Ward P. Christie in a speech to the American Society of Civil Engineers, quoted in W. Starrett, 87.

57. On the "cost-plus" basis of George A. Fuller, see Bruegmann, 484, note 63 and on other contractors, "The Skyline Builders," 95.

58. W. Starrett, 92.

59. John P. Carmody, "The Empire State Building. X. Field Organization Methods," *Architectural Forum* (April 1931): 475–506.

60. Carmody, 497.

61. P. Starrett, 296.

62. "Skyline Builders," 96.

63. P. Starrett, 298–299.

64. P. Starrett, 295.

65. P. Starrett, 299.

66. P. Starrett, 299–300.

67. That is the figure used throughout Starrett Brothers and Eken records.

68. In 1927, at Bill Starrett's urging, the company formed a subsidiary, Starrett Brothers Corporation, to act as a development partner in some of their buildings: the 40 Wall and 63 Wall Street office buildings, as well as the Carew Tower were partially financed by the company. The company lost nearly $200,000 on Cincinnati, and probably even more the other ventures. P. Starrett, 308, 314.

69. P. Starrett, 308. William Starrett died in 1932, as Paul observed in his 1937 autobiography, "a victim of overwork and long nervous strain," 316.

70. An account of the ceremonies appeared in the New York *Sun*, May 1, 1931 in an article by Edwin C. Hill. From a clipping in the Empire State Building scrapbooks, number 5, Special Collections, Avery Architectural and Fine Arts Library, Columbia University. The list of speakers was noted in "Outline for Opening Ceremonies May 1st," du Pont Papers at Hagley Museum and Library, Longwood Mss., 229-15, Empire State Inc., 1931, folder 52, III.

71. In 1928, when the vacancy rate began to rise, there were calls for a moratorium on new construction, but the following year, the vacancy rate dropped to 4.8 percent, starts were again strong, and banks and bond houses were eager lenders. See Gordon MacDonald, *Office Building Construction, Manhattan 1901–1953* (New York: Real Estate Board of New York, 1952), 6.

72. William Starrett declared his optimism in a speech to an industry organization, stating: "I think it is altogether reasonable to predict that building activities for the coming year will be materially better than last year and that there will be a reasonable degree of activity from this time forward." Clipping, New York *Evening Post*, January 2, 1930, n.p.

73. The vacancy rate for office space in Manhattan in 1934 was 24.8 percent, according to MacDonald, op. cit., 6.

74. Report to Stockholders, April 1932, Hagley Museum and Library, Longwood Mss., 229-15, Empire State Inc., 1932–33, folder 77.

75. By the end of the decade, the tower was still nearly two-thirds vacant. The initial schedule of rents projected in October 1929 had estimated the annual income of the building at $7,961,580, but in the first ten years of operation, the total rents were less than one third of that sum. The stockholders had to cover these mounting deficiencies, first through the sacrifice of their initial capital investment, then with cash to meet operating expenses.

76. The number, twenty-one months, is different than my count of twenty months; it may refer to August 1929 through April 1931, or perhaps September 1929 through May 1931.

"A STORY A DAY": ENGINEERING THE WORK

Donald Friedman

SETTING RECORDS

This essay introduces a unique description of the Empire State as seen through of its builders' eyes while they were involved with the work. Their *Notes on Construction of Empire State Building* is not architectural history, but it has the immediacy and detail that only a first-hand account can convey. *Notes* discusses aspects of the building that are rarely considered. Rather than viewing the building as a triumph of architectural and engineering design or of sheer size, the authors of this fascinating document saw it as the result of a process. The writers' pride shows as much in their detailed explanations as in the rather cosmically oriented conclusion, where the *Notes* looked to temper seventy pages of construction details with thoughts about posterity. The writers' opinion of the significance of their work slips in: the Empire State is a "majestic symbol of the enterprise and efficiency of our age."

Spectacularly tall and architecturally distinguished, the Empire State represents the culmination of the skyscraper boom of the 1920s, but the most remarkable aspect of the building—one that has not been surpassed by a younger, taller, or bigger building—is the speed of its construction. The most lasting statistical record of the Empire State is one based on logistics—the expertise of Starrett Brothers and Eken, the builders.

Although the Empire State was the tallest building in the world for over forty years, and height was the focus of public interest and hyperbole, its height was less revolutionary than press releases intimated. At the end of construction in 1930, 1,045 feet to the main roof and 1,252 feet to the top of the mooring mast and observation deck structure were records, but they were not significant leaps in scale. When the Woolworth Building was completed in 1913, the tallest building in the world at 792 feet, it was almost 30 percent taller than the previous record holder, the Singer Building. The Chrysler Building, next in line as the world's tallest, was over 30 percent taller than the Woolworth. The Empire State, by contrast, was less than 20 percent higher than the Chrysler.

Most people consider the Empire State a beautiful work, regardless of its height. Beauty is, of course, entirely subjective. Any attempt to classify buildings as the "World's Most Beautiful" in the manner of the "World's Tallest" is likely to start an argument that will leave no one satisfied. (Even height, a seemingly objective criterion, has provoked arguments: highest usable floor versus highest building structure versus top of spires, antennas, or flagpoles.)

The Empire State is one of a series of very tall buildings built in the late 1920s in a modern style, with its interior organized around efficient elevator use and access to windows for the tenants. The style, detailing, and interior planning of the Empire State, while well thought out, were not exceptional at the time.

The unrivaled fact about the Empire State is that it was completed, from its foundations to occupancy, in less than one year. That is an enviable construction speed for any large building, but incredible for such a tall building on a constrained site in the middle of congested midtown Manhattan. The speed of construction relative to the size of the project has rarely been attained anywhere and is still considered to be a worthy goal for tall-building construction. Blaming modern safety requirements for a slower rate of construction today is grossly inaccurate. As described in the *Notes*, safety for both the laborers on site and the public nearby was a prime concern of the builders, who took precautions similar to those later required by law.

STRUCTURE:
FRAME, FLOORS, FACADES

The basic structural form of the Empire State reflects the technology of its time—the lessons learned from the design and construction of thousands of smaller steel-framed buildings during the first thirty years of the twentieth century. No single part of the base construction was exceptional. The steel frame, concrete floor slabs, and mechanical systems that make the building usable all were similar to other buildings, although significantly larger.

The physical structure of the Empire State can be divided into three major elements: the frame, the floors, and the façade. Other elements (for example, the elevators or the plumbing) are essential to the daily functioning of the skyscraper, but not to our recognition of it as a building. Without elevators, it would be awkward to reach the eightieth floor, but there would not be an eightieth floor without floor slabs.

The frame of the Empire State consists of steel sections riveted together. This was not the first method of building tall buildings, nor the last, but at the time of construction it had been the most successful method for over thirty-five years. In the portion of the *Notes* called "The Fascination of Speed," structural steel comes first, and not only for chronological accuracy. The other three "pacemakers"—building elements that determined the construction schedule—were the floor slabs and the two major elements of the exterior façades. Not only did the erection of these elements depend directly on the erection of the steel frame, but their placement was less obvious to the passers-by. Anyone, regardless of construction expertise, could see the frame extending higher into the sky, and judge the speed of construction. William Starrett's description of the process reflected the public fascination with steel framing: "Columns commence to stand up like magically produced trees, those farthest from the derrick first, then here and there a panel of steel. Almost as you watch, you notice the connecting of the panels, and in a day or two a whole tier of beams . . . ."[1] Constructing the interior floors and the exterior cladding was tame by comparison.

Ordinary floor beams and smaller columns (the columns toward the top of the building) at the Empire State all have the familiar "I" shape known as a wide-flange section. Design of a floor beam is independent of which floor the beam is part of. In contrast, the design of columns varies with the loads, increasing toward the base. At upper floors, there is not a great difference in size between the wide-flange sections used for beams and those used for columns, and at the middle and lower floors, the beams are identical to those at the top. At the middle floors, the columns are heavier wide-flange sections. At the bottom of the building, the largest wide-flange sections available in 1930 were too small to carry the load of the floors above, so these columns are built up of relatively small sections riveted together. This technique had been used before large wide-flange sections were available, but gradually became rare during the 1920s as steel mills produced larger and larger sections. As described in the *Notes*, some of the built-up columns at the base were the heaviest pieces of steel used in building construction at that time. This is simply one of an enormous number of statistical firsts, but one with a direct link to the building's exceptional character: the size of the columns is a rough guide to the height of the building.

The steel arrived on site with connections already attached, so the pieces could be immediately lifted into place and riveted to the already-erected surrounding members. Steel columns typically came, and still come, in two-story-high sections, with a splice at the bottom, beam connections in the middle, and beam connections and a splice at the top. The frame was thus assembled two stories at a time, with the new two-story-high columns and the two floors of beams that fill in between the columns making up a "tier." When all of the connections for a tier were complete, the columns for the next tier above were set in place, starting the cycle again.

The problems faced by the engineers in the office of Homer G. Balcom, designers of the steel frame, while not entirely ordinary, were soluble. The frame had to carry gravity loads of the weight of the building and its occupants, had to resist the sideways push of wind, and had to provide attachment for the various mechanical systems. Increasing the scale of the building required clever and precise engineering, but not any major changes in intent or process. The mooring mast, with its airship load (which was unique to the Empire State) was not a major concern in structural design because of the size of the load relative to the size of the building. The lateral load from a moored airship would be 50 tons; the lateral load from wind blowing on the north face of the building would be well over 2,000 tons. Compared to the bracing required to keep the building upright when subjected to wind load, the additional bracing required by the mooring mast was almost negligible.

One peculiarity of very tall buildings came to light during the course of the work: they tend to be slightly shorter than the builders think they are. A survey done before steel erection by E. B. Lovell established the elevation below grade of the column base plates. As each tier of steel was erected, its height was known in advance, so when all of the steel was erected, finding the elevation of any given floor from grade should have been a matter of simple arithmetic. Mechanics, the branch of applied physics that provides the theoretical background for structural engineering, explains why floor heights were lower than expected: everything moves under load. Steel columns, symbols of solidity, become shorter when loaded, and as the load increases, so does the "squashing" of the columns. The first-tier columns measured immediately after erection would be the same length they were in the shop, but as each floor was built, and the "dead load" accumulated in the form of the floor slabs, the exterior walls, and the interior partitions and plaster, the columns became steadily shorter.

Because steel is very stiff, the effect, while small, is measurable over a building eighty-six stories high. Starrett Brothers and Eken noticed this as they were trying to coordinate all the building trades. In December 1930 the eighty-fifth floor was reported to be more than 6 inches lower than expected, most likely by the elevator subcontractor attempting to complete the elevator banks.[2] Elevator machinery must be tuned to precise distances, and therefore requires careful surveying. People working in other trades, such as the masons setting the exterior limestone, would not have noticed the discrepancy, because they deal only with fractions of a floor's height at any given time. A discrepancy of .007 inch at one floor is easily overlooked, while one of 6 inches is not. Column shortening requires some retuning of the elevator controllers, but creates no other problems or danger. It is a graphic reminder that skyscrapers are more than masses of statistics about size; they are qualitatively different from ordinary buildings.

During construction (or when the interior partitions and ceilings are removed for tenant alterations), the floor slabs are plainly visible. In the Empire State, 4-inch-thick slabs of concrete span roughly 7 feet between steel beams. The type of slab, concrete made with coal cinders as aggregate and reinforced with draped wire mesh, is peculiar to the first half of the twentieth century. The mesh is key to how the slabs work. The tops of the steel beams are 2 inches below the top of the slab. The wire mesh rests on top of the beams and then sags, or drapes down, so that half-way between the beams it is less than an inch from the bottom of the slab. The mesh forms a series of strong catenaries spanning between the beams and carrying the floor loads like the cables of a suspension bridge. The slab itself is lightweight and weak; the strength of concrete is not important when the concrete is only spanning 2 inches between wires in the mesh.

Draped mesh slabs are strong, lightweight, fireproof, and, because they use cinders to supply bulk, inexpensive. They were built by erecting a wood form between and around the steel beams, unrolling wire mesh over the beams, and placing the concrete. The word "arches" in *Notes* refers to the concrete floor slabs, a carryover from the previous generation of high-rise construction with its terra-cotta-arch floors. The draped mesh floor had been refined for more than twenty years before its use at the Empire State and could not readily be improved, which is why there are relatively few floor references in the *Notes*.

In contrast to the rather typical slabs, the façades were specially planned and designed with speed and efficiency of construction in mind. The cooperation between the designers and the builders was part of the effort to bend all parts of the building process to the construction schedule. Shreve, Lamb, and Harmon were commercial architects, as concerned with building and their clients' wishes as with fine points of art. H. G. Balcom, the structural engineer, came from a background in steel fabrication and railroad construction—a well-known route to a practical outlook and an aim to build quickly. The architects of many of the buildings erected during the 1920s' skyscraper boom were known more for their commercial instincts. Only now, looking back on the buildings those designers created, can it be seen that planning for rapid construction did not exclude attractive and functional results. The fact that the designers allowed the concerns of the builders to influence their work is a point in their favor.

The most significant influence of construction technique on architectural design can be seen in the façades. The need for rapid erection influenced the details of the façades and the methods used for fabrication, as Carol Willis describes.

The exterior of the Empire State is a curtain wall; its nonstructural exterior cladding functions to keep weather out. Unlike the bearing walls of the earliest skyscrapers in the 1870s and 1880s, curtain walls do not need to be heavy because they are supported by the steel frame at each floor, which eliminates any significant gravity load in the masonry. Wind blowing on the building is resisted by the walls, which carry the load to the steel frame. A standard curtain wall of the 1920s was face masonry (brick, terra-cotta, or cut stone) fastened to common brick and ordinarily built as a continuous plane with "holes" for windows. No distinction was made between the masonry above and below windows (the "spandrel panels") and the continuous masonry vertical strips between windows (the

"piers"). The windows and the spandrels were supported against movement in or out of the plane of the wall by the piers, while each portion of the wall supported its own weight vertically down to the steel at the next floor.

The Empire State curtain wall was a more advanced design, dividing the wall into separate standardized pieces, each with its own function. The piers are continuous limestone panels with a common brick backing. The spandrel panels consist of decorative aluminum outside a common brick backing, extending from the bottom of each floor structure to the base of the window. The window frames extend from the top of the spandrel panels to the bottom of the structure of the next floor, which is covered by the bottom of the aluminum panel. To tie the various elements together and provide lateral bracing to the windows, strips of stainless steel run vertically from floor to floor at the juncture of the piers and the window/spandrel panel lines.

This design contributed to the speed of construction. The limestone piers consist of a very large number of identical pieces, without side connections, and the stainless steel strips hide the joints between the piers and the spandrel panels, also eliminating the need for any sideways connection. The detailing of the limestone therefore could be much simpler than in ordinary walls, where each piece required connections side to side as well as up and down. The hidden side edges of the stone panels were not finished; leaving them rough had no visible effect, and eliminated half of the edge finishing work. This system cleanly separates the function of enclosure from the semi-structural function of self-weight and wind support. Curtain walls consisting mostly of glass sheets, which had been built as early as the 1910s and became popular in tall buildings in the 1950s, carry this separation to its extreme. In glass walls, the panes enclose the building interior while the metal mullions carry the wind loads. The Empire State was an important, but not unprecedented, step in the evolution of curtain walls from continuous planes of masonry to sheets of glass.

In using a modern design, the architects and builders recognized the importance of wall construction to their scheme. R. H. Shreve wrote that "to a great extent the form and proportions of the structure have influenced the development of" the wall construction detail.[3]

The method of supporting the curtain walls on the steel frame was unusual. Ordinary curtain walls of the time were supported on steel shelf angles, which are hung from the beams at the edge of the building and allowed for adjustment, but required many individual pieces: the shelves and the hanging clips. The Empire State had an extra beam outboard of the ordinary edge beam, which was erected as a part of the steel frame and directly supported the brick backing for the piers and spandrel panels, eliminating the laborious work of adjusting the shelves.

The erection sequence for the wall reflected all of these physical innovations. It also moved as much work as possible off exterior scaffolding (where façade construction had traditionally taken place) and into the building. The stainless steel strips were placed first, secured to the steel frame. The aluminum spandrel panels and limestone veneer were then set in place, then the brick backing built behind. Once the windows were installed on top of the backing, the inside space was enclosed from the weather, so that interior finish work could begin. The normal link between construction schedules for veneer and the backing had been severed.

These innovations created the distinctive appearance of the building, with gleaming stainless steel lines set off against the medium gray limestone and the dark gray aluminum panels. They also sped the construction of the structural steel, for once the material weight of the wall materials was set, the additional edge beams could be sized and included in the steel package, eliminating the need for coordination between the steel fabrication and the detailing of the façade.

BUILDING SYSTEMS

Like all modern buildings, the Empire State is far more complicated than a simple enclosure of space. Threading through the interior of the building are conduits carrying electric service to outlets for tenants and to built-in equipment, steam pipes feeding radiators, ducts carrying fresh air to the interior spaces of the large lower floors, and pipes to supply and service restrooms. Fifty-eight elevators service various floors, requiring machine rooms containing motors and controllers at seven different floors.

The engineers designing the mechanical systems faced well-known problems, which were increased by the scale of the project. They needed to pump water for use in the building to tanks at the twenty-first, thirty-first, forty-sixth, sixty-fourth, and eighty-fifth floors, to design the elevators that accounted for the

weight of the cables in the shafts, and to step down the voltage of the electric power from the mains and subdivide it for each floor. They had to take in, filter, and distribute air for the ventilation ducts without creating excessive noise or strong drafts. None of these issues was new, but the standard solutions had to be adapted to the extraordinary conditions.

The design of the electrical system gives a good example of the effects of sheer size on standard mechanical design. In the *Notes*, the effects are best described by the superintendent for the electrical subcontractor. From his point of view, there was little difference between the problems caused by the size of the building and those caused by the schedule. His account therefore combines design and constructibility issues, but it is still very informative. In a smaller skyscraper, the high-voltage power provided by the mains under the streets is stepped down to an intermediate voltage in the basement, and an intermediate voltage riser extends up through the building. At each floor, a second transformer located in an electrical "closet" at the riser location steps the voltage down to the standard 110/220 volts used for tenant services. This system was well tested by 1930, and is still in use. At the Empire State, the ordinary system would have resulted in extremely large intermediate risers and many conduits extending from the closet out across each floor. Two changes in design by Meyer Strong & Jones, the mechanical engineers, solved both problems by effectively treating the building as several smaller buildings combined. First, they used two risers, placed at opposite ends of the elevator core, to reduce the extent of local feeder conduit on each floor. Second, they used high-voltage feeders to transformers on the forty-first and eighty-fourth floors, supplementing the transformers in the sub-basement. Adding high-voltage equipment on upper floors (ordinarily confined to the basement) at upper floors kept the risers to a manageable size. The two design decisions taken together effectively turned the building into six smaller buildings—two side by side, stacked three high.[4]

Minor refinements of standard practice had the cumulative effect of speeding the electrical installation. Distribution conduit for ceiling fixtures runs within the structural floor slabs and ordinarily bent up toward the slab top at each floor beam and bend down toward the slab bottom at each fixture. At the Empire State, the conduit runs straight, requiring the use of deeper-than-usual junction boxes at the fixtures and at intersections of conduit, but eliminating the labor of bending the conduit out of the horizontal plane. Straight conduit also sped the slowest step in the local electrical installation—pulling the wire through the conduit, since every bend in conduit slows pulling the wire and provides a point where the wire can stick. Similar stories could be told about the installation of piping, elevators, and ventilation equipment. In each case, two primary problems competed for the attention of the designers and the builders: how to ensure that the systems functioned as well as in smaller buildings, and how to simplify ordinary practice to keep construction on schedule.

SYSTEMATIZING CONSTRUCTION

Logistics always have been the key to the success of large construction projects. Designers can spend years making details as perfect as possible, but without a proper plan of construction, the time is wasted. At the Empire State, where time was compressed, a thorough plan for construction was even more crucial.

Unlike the well-defined problems facing designers, builders have to deal with external conditions beyond their control: availability of materials, fluctuations in labor and material prices, and most important, transportation. Moving materials to the correct location, removing refuse, and getting laborers to their work can be the most difficult tasks in the organization of a large project, especially when access is limited. A building under construction does not have the full complement of finished stairs and elevators, well-defined and clearly marked hallways, or even necessarily a front door. The common problems of building construction are exacerbated further by the congestion in a city center and have through history: one of the oldest known construction laws is the prohibition on daytime passage of carts bearing building materials through the streets of imperial Rome. Modern technology may have improved the efficiency of transport and the speed of construction, but it has also increased the quantities of materials that need to be carried to a building site and the complexity of the work that needs to be performed. By 1909, the strain of tall-building construction was already apparent to the editorial writers of the *New York Globe*:

A city building is constructed from hand to mouth. Little can be stored on the job. The narrow, crowded streets of a city like New York leave no room for storage outside, even if you do take up a third of the street, as the law allows. If the kickers, who raise such a row (as *The Globe* did a couple of years ago) about these obstructions, would have to try it themselves, they'd perhaps be more sympathetic.[5]

Twenty years later, the importance of site organization and transportation was so well understood that it was no longer editorial fodder, but rather the basis of Starrett Brothers and Eken's business. If logistics had become the overriding concern during construction, then a successful contracting business could be built on providing better organization—on systematizing the well-known chaos of a construction site.

It is not an exaggeration to say that every aspect of the construction process at the Empire State was driven by the need for efficient transportation. To understand why, it is necessary to look at the problems facing the builders from their point of view.

The records for the steel erection show that the schedule was, in the language of modern construction management, "front-loaded"—that is, more than half of the work was scheduled to be performed before the midpoint of the scheduled time. The pace at the beginning was more important than the pace at the end, because time lost from early mistakes cannot be made up without disproportionately increasing in speed.

The structural frame of the Empire State consists of roughly 57,000 tons of steel. The shape of the building and the size of the columns combined to front-load the erection of the steel. In accordance with the New York City zoning law, the building sets back repeatedly from the edges of its lot, making the lower floors substantially larger in area than the upper floors. At the same time, the columns in the lower floors are far heavier than those above. Both of these properties concentrate the weight of steel in the lower floors, a point noted in press statements about the amount of steel erected by different dates. The boundaries of the steel timeline were placement of the first structural steel columns in the lowest basement on April 7, 1930, and the topping out of the main building frame on September 22, 1930. On July 9, roughly halfway through the erection time, the steel tonnage in place was almost 30,000 tons, or roughly half the total.[6] Half of the steel, however, only brought the frame up to the twentieth floor. On August 1, roughly 46,000 tons or 80 percent of the steel was in place, with the top of the frame at the fiftieth floor.[7] In short, the top 40 percent (36 floors) of the building's height used only 20 percent of the steel.

The labor in steel construction is concentrated in

making the connections. The number of connections at the thirtieth floor is the same as at the seventieth floor, but the columns at the lower floors are heavier and therefore require more effort to move and position. A schedule based solely on the number of connections to be made—the number of rivets to be driven—would not reflect the fact that more effort was required to erect the lower floors. If the steel erection had lagged seriously behind schedule at the beginning of the work, it would have been almost impossible to compensate later on. For example, the steel for the first twenty floors took roughly three and a half days per floor to erect. If the work had been slightly slower, and required four and a half days per floor, the remaining work would have had to average one working day per floor. Since one day per floor was the peak erection speed reached during construction, a slight reduction in speed for the first twenty floors would have required weekend work or moving back the October 1 deadline.

The construction industry has accepted speed benchmarks. Paul Starrett later wrote that in 1930 he knew from experience that erecting three and a half floors of steel frame in a week was the standard pace, and that it was too slow for the construction schedule at the Empire State. Other standards of the time were five floors per week for common brick walls and between three and five stories per week for stone veneer on exterior walls, also too slow for the project.[8] These standards were much faster than those used a generation earlier, before the industrialization of building sites. They were not substantially improved upon for the rest of the twentieth century, because they represent the speed with which work can be performed given the inherent difficulties in movement around and within construction sites.

Between 1900 and 1930 the building construction industry was reorganized, in large part because of the strain of constructing very large buildings that were internally more complex than their predecessors. Ideas about industrial management and efficiency being applied in factories were brought to the construction process, but the actual labor of construction was (and is) resistant to the methods used to increase industrial efficiency. Methods used to increase efficiency in a factory (assembly lines, division of labor into small tasks, time-and-motion studies) could not be applied to skilled trades that had to be performed in specific orders in specific, difficult-to-reach locations.

The organization of the construction business was not so resistant to modern pressures. The time in question saw the beginning of the modern construction manager—the company that oversees all of the trades without actually performing any of the work. These companies grew at the expense of general contractors—companies that handled one or more major trades while subcontracting out portions of the work. In the case of Starrett Brothers and Eken, a general contracting company was transforming itself into a construction manager. At the Empire State, nearly half of the labor was supplied by subcontractors. This would not have been acceptable for a reputable general contractor in 1900. As construction management became popular after 1945, the percentage of laborers supplied by the main building company shrank toward zero.

The process of replacing the old hierarchy of labor with one of management was seen as a necessary revolution in 1907. According to the *New York Herald*:

> The old-fashioned piecemeal system of building is a hard institution to go up against, but something must be done or high grade building will become such a luxury that those who can indulge in it won't, for they won't have to. Disappointments are still in store for the owner who builds on the old-fashioned plan.
>
> A student of industrial conditions, having knowledge of the methods used in manufacturing and in merchandising, would observe that one invariable circumstance surrounds the examples of building construction where time has been unnecessarily consumed and cost has been very great, and that is the absence of a direct control over all the operations which enter into the production of the product.[9]

Twenty years after these general observations about the need for centralized organization, the revolution had taken place. Paul Starrett was one of the beneficiaries of this change. In his autobiography, *Changing the Skyline*, he showed as much pride in his role in establishing the modern construction system as he did in any physical results of his work. His account of the interview with the board of the Empire State that secured the job for his company is fascinating for its emphasis. In describing how he persuaded the owners, Starrett quickly ran through his company's technical qualifications (for example, they had just completed the New York Life Building, a project of great complexity) before describing the issues he saw as key: speed and efficiency. He was proud of shocking his interviewers by bragging that his company had no equipment on hand, would build from scratch any specialized tools needed for the project, and would do no work that could be subcontracted.[10] Today, with construction management as an established field, none of these points is shocking.

What was impressive about the Empire State was the builders' organization of the work, by which men and materials were present when and where they were needed.

TRANSPORTING MATERIALS

The problem of transport within the site in effect existed before the site itself. In order to meet the owners' schedule, Starrett Brothers and Eken had to demolish the old Waldorf-Astoria Hotel as efficiently as they had to construct the new building. Accelerating demolition is more difficult than speeding construction, because demolition is inherently more dangerous and therefore allows for fewer innovations. It must be was carried out largely by hand because the process of taking a building apart is one of intentional destabilization that can result in collapse if done too rapidly or with too much force. The contractor rarely has much structural information on the building to be demolished, and this lack of knowledge translates into slow and methodical work. Rather than using wrecking balls in areas where experience dictated hand-work, Starrett Brothers and Eken concentrated on speeding demolition through the rapid removal of debris.

The Waldorf-Astoria Hotel consisted of four interlocking buildings, erected between 1892 and 1897. Although all had metal framing (a mix of cast iron, wrought iron, and steel), they were much heavier than later buildings, containing far more masonry per cubic foot of enclosed volume. Much of the masonry was in thick exterior walls and interior partitions. Because the hotel was built before concrete became popular in the United States, even the floors were terra-cotta tile. Breaking up all of the masonry was probably easier than demolishing concrete would have been, but the sheer volume of debris posed a problem. In addition, the steel frames of the hotel buildings had to be cut apart and carted away.

Starrett Brothers and Eken cut shafts through the buildings from the top to the first floor, drove trucks into the buildings, parked them directly below the shafts, and filled them with debris by dumping it from above. This method, while not unique, was the most advanced transport that could be readily used during demolition, because it reduced interference by traffic.

While many items were salvaged during demolition for sentimental reasons or material value, the builders kept four relatively new elevator cabs for a more practical purpose. They were of no use in the new building—elevators are built for a specific shaft, and cannot be permanently reused without a refitting process as involved as building new cabs—but they were successfully used for temporary transportation, getting laborers up to the new floors where they were needed.

After demolition, Starrett Brothers and Eken handled the common construction transportation problems with a variety of creative techniques. Transportation details are always site-specific, dependent on the particular work and site. At the Empire State, horizontal transportation outside the site, which was largely beyond the control of the builders, was handled traditionally. Horizontal transportation—the use of a small railroad within the building—used the most radical innovations. Vertical transportation was by necessity more challenging than on most sites, because traditional methods were simply inadequate to the scale of the new building and the speed of construction.

A series of materials hoists were set up within the building in temporary shafts created by leaving out portions of the permanent floor structure. (The shafts were later filled in.) The special slab work required by running the shafts inside the building paid for itself because the lateral supports for the lifting equipment that temporary external shafts required were unnecessary.

Six hoists were used—two dedicated to concrete and four to general materials and carrying tracks for the temporary, narrow-gauge railroad built for on-site horizontal movement. The hoists were not new technology, but were an interestingly complex response to a simple need, getting materials to the laborers.

The hoist shafts were extended upwards during the work, following the rising height of the building. Because the lifting machinery for the hoists was primitive compared with that required for safe use by passengers, it could be changed with little design effort. The motors used were swapped as the hoist shafts became taller, with larger motors used as the shaft lengths approached their maximum lengths of eighty-two stories. An additional shaft was supplied for disposal of the debris (called "dirt") produced during construction. The method of disposal resembled that used during the Waldorf-Astoria demolition, including a direct feed into trucks parked on the ground floor of the building, but the chute built in the new building was lined with steel plate to protect the surrounding floor structure.

The method of to-site delivery of materials was the standard of the day: they were brought long-distance to New York by train, and delivered to the site from freight depots by truck. The difficulty with the system was that Fifth Avenue is in the middle of Manhattan Island, so any route that could be used by trucks would pass through midtown traffic. The standard method for avoiding delays in this circumstance was (and remains) to schedule deliveries for the dawn or predawn hours, when traffic is lighter. Starrett Brothers and Eken took a more radical approach: through the use of unique on-site transportation methods and rare, on-site concrete production, the delivery of material to the location of work within the site was insulated from the schedule of deliveries. Organization and rapid site-interior movement made up for the lack of material storage space.

The scheme for materials handling was divided into three parts: handling bulk materials (e.g., brick or electrical conduit), handling fabricated materials (e.g., steel or limestone), and handling concrete.

Materials other than steel were delivered to the site by ordinary trucks, which drove into the building off 33rd and 34th Streets. Common brick, sand, cement, gypsum, and cinders were dumped through holes in the first floor into hoppers in the basements, which were then used for distribution. Cars in the narrow-gauge railroad were placed below the hoppers and loaded, then rolled to the concrete plants or to the proper hoist for lifting to the floor where they were required. More fragile materials, such as the exterior limestone and the terra-cotta block used for interior partitions, were unloaded from the trucks traditionally, by hand, and stacked by spurs of the narrow-gauge railroad. They could then be loaded into flatcars to be rolled into the hoists.

Notes records "nearly 500" truck loads of all types on the peak day, an extreme number for movement within the floor-plan of a single building. The key to this achievement was the speed of unloading the bulk material trucks, which in turn depended on the hoists and narrow-gauge railroad.

Concrete formed a category of its own because, once mixed, it has a short usable life, and it was needed in such large amounts for the floor slabs. Treated like the bulk materials—sand, cinders, cement, and wire reinforcing—it was delivered to the site in bulk. The method chosen for concrete batching and delivery was the most involved process in materials trans-

portation on the site. Once the materials that make up concrete (cement, sand, aggregate, and water) are mixed, the chemical reaction that causes the cement to set up begins, and cannot be stopped until the mixture is hard. To eliminate delays from outside transportation, the concrete for the floors of the Empire State was batched in two plants in the basement. The materials stored in bins were measured into the batching plants, mixed with water, and then placed into buckets to be carried to the appropriate floor by one of the two dedicated hoists. Each bucket held almost exactly one cubic yard (the standard measure for wet concrete); more than 300 cubic yards of concrete was needed for the slabs of a single tower floor.

Horizontal movement of materials within the site was handled through the innovative narrow-gauge railroad. These railroads, referred to by the builders as "industrial railroad," formed loops on every floor as it was built and expedited the movement of supplies from the vertical hoists to where the work was being performed. The tracks laid on the lower floors, where concrete was being mixed and truckloads of other materials sorted and broken up into usable bundles, remained through the construction. The tracks on the office floors were in place long enough to complete the shell of the building, and were then removed to permit the construction of interior partitions. The tracks were moved up to the next floor under construction and reused.

The complicated and expensive rail system was devised to compensate for the extremely rapid schedule and the relatively large floor area. The lower floors were 198 by 425 feet and the tower floors were 134 by 186 feet in plan. For previous tall buildings with smaller floor plans, the effort of laying and taking up the rail would have outweighed the advantages.

The rail system was the heart of the materials-transportation organization. Efficient use of the hoists demanded that the materials on the receiving end (the upper floors) be taken from the hoist to the point of use as quickly as possible. The number of photographs of the rails in *Notes* suggests that the builders felt this was the most visible aspect of their dedication to efficiency. Intelligent organization is not very photogenic; a railroad (however small) inside a building under construction is.

TRANSPORTING PEOPLE

The daily movement of laborers from the sidewalk to and from the floors on which they worked was the greatest problem of vertical transportation within the building as it rose. At most sites, each laborer made four such trips: up in the morning, down at lunch, up in the afternoon, and down at the end of the day. Starrett Brothers and Eken eliminated nearly half of these by providing well-run, inexpensive lunch counters within the building. There were eventually five lunch counters, added one at a time as the building reached its height.

The temporary elevators set up to move laborers were organized as the permanent elevators would be, with cars serving different zones. The arrangement is not a coincidence: there are very few methods of organizing the rapid movement of people using a system, like elevators, fixed in extent and capacity. The construction elevators were a variation on zoned express service: a system of elevators arranged in groups that serve progressively higher floors, the first group stopping at every floor from the ground to the lowest floor served by the second group; the second group stops at the ground floor, runs express past the floors served by the first group, and then stops at every floor up to the lowest served by the third group, and so on. Because every group of zoned elevators has to run separately to the ground, this system is less efficient than true express cars which drop people off at upper floors (often called "sky lobbies"), where they transfer to local elevators to their destination. In a true express system, the local elevator shafts can be "stacked," using the same shaft location for local service at different levels. Nevertheless, zoned express service is used for the majority of passenger elevators in high-rise buildings (including the Empire State) because it does not require passengers to switch elevators.

Standard construction elevators stop at every floor. This approach at the Empire State would have been a bottleneck in efficient transportation given the height of the building and the large numbers of laborers. The solution used zoned service without the expresses. A set of elevators handled traffic from the ground to a transfer point. Anyone continuing above got out and transferred to the elevator for the next zone. The type of elevator and the number of zones changed as the work proceeded. The zoned temporary system provided faster movement of the workers—a trade-off that Starrett Brothers and Eken must have thought worthwhile.

Two ordinary construction elevators (open cars called "mine cage lifts") were provided first. These move extremely rapidly and, like the materials hoists, could be extended upwards quickly and easily as the work demanded. The upward extension of the construction elevators was performed at night to avoid interfering with construction of the building. As the building grew taller, the bottom floor served by the mine cages was gradually raised. Four temporary shafts were created by leaving out portions of the permanent floor structure, as with the shafts for the materials hoists. The first replacements for the mine cage cars were the elevators salvaged from the Waldorf-Astoria. These were used and extended upwards in the lower shafts previously used by the mine cage cars when they were moved for upper-floor service.

The permanent elevators were constructed by the Otis Elevator Company as the other work on the building proceeded. As some of the new elevators were completed and made usable (with temporary, disposable finishes inside the permanent cars), they were used to serve the lower levels. By the end of the frame erection there were three types of service: temporary use of the permanent elevators at the bottom of the building, temporary use of the salvaged elevators in the middle of the building, and the mine-cage elevators at the top of the building. These can be seen as three bands moving up the building: first the mine cages, which started at the bottom and eventually moved all the way to the top; then the salvaged cars, which replaced the mine cages at the bottom and never made it all the way to the top; then the permanent cars, which replaced the salvaged cars at the bottom, ran as far as halfway up the building by the end of steel erection, and eventually took over all service.

The interwoven switching of transportation service seen with the elevators was a standard feature of large civil engineering projects, as roads or railroads were rerouted to keep people moving while construction took place. It is rare in building construction because erecting most buildings is not a transportation problem as long as sufficient time and storage space exist to buffer the movement of people and materials through the site.

ORGANIZING THE STEEL

The extreme measures taken to avoid delay in constructing the steel frame illustrate detailed systematization as a response to deadline pressure. The amount of steel used in the building, while large for one building, was not a dominating percentage of the country's capacity for rolling and fabricating structural steel. Rather than awarding the steel fabricating contract to the low-bidder, Starrett Brothers and Eken signed the two lowest qualified bidders and divided the building into horizontal slices, with alternating sections supplied by the American Bridge Company and the McClintic-Marshall Company. These sections ranged in height from two to eight stories or, more accurately, from one to four tiers.

One firm, Post & McCord, performed the steel erection because this process could not be logically divided. Dividing the fabrication contract gave each of the two firms more time to perform their jobs; dividing the erection contract would have created more work from the coordination of switching crane and riveting crews back and forth.

Each piece of steel was meant for a specific location. In addition, each steel member was defined by crane (locating the steel on the floor plan), by tier (locating the floor within one of the horizontal slices, and thus determining which fabricator was responsible for the piece and when it was needed for the erection schedule), and by floor. Structural steel is detailed for fabrication by shop drawings, which are the fabricator's interpretation of the structural engineer's somewhat schematic drawings. Shop drawings are divided into two types: piece drawings that show the exact location of every rivet or bolt, and erection drawings that show where each piece goes along with any information required for proper sequencing. The Empire State erection plans were complex, and included drawings not usually required, such the erection schedule drawing prepared by Post & McCord, a good example of the complexity of the steel erection organization (see Fig. 1). This single drawing graphically shows six independent organizational variables as well as several dependent variables. The center of the drawing is a diagram of the building frame showing all of the columns and beams on the east face of the building (called the "east elevation"). The floor-to-floor heights (needed for crane rigging) are supplied in the center of the elevation. To the right of the elevation are two floor plans, one of the first through fifth floors and the other of the twenty-second through seventy-first floors, which supply the boundaries between the nine cranes lifting areas (lettered A through H and K) and the column designations (numbered 1 through 220). Cranes A, D, E, and H were used from the basement levels through twenty-first floor, and then discontinued.

Immediately to the left of the elevation is a series of numbers representing the weight of steel (in tons) in each tier. The numbers gradually decrease from bottom to top of the building, even on "identical" tiers, because of the decrease in weight of the columns. The heaviest tier is the one containing the first two basement levels below grade. The elevation shows the curb height on the right, over thirty feet from the lowest tier of steel.

To the left of the tonnage marks are three related series: the fabricator (A for American Bridge, M for McClintic-Marshall), the floor number (with 86 shown as the roof), and the tier number. The floor numbers alone would have given the necessary information, but providing all three reduced the possibility of error.

Finally, to the left of the floor data, is a series of dates, organized by tier. The dates described as "required" were the dates that had been set to keep to the schedule of delivering the completed steel frame on October 1, 1930. From left to right, they are the date that the structural engineer, H.G. Balcom, was required to issue the design data for the given tier ("INFO"), the date the data was actually received by Post & McCord, the date that Post & McCord was required to order the steel from the proper fabricator ("ADV. BILLS"), the date that the steel was actually ordered, the date that the approved shop drawings had to be sent to the fabricators ("DRWG"), the date that the drawings were actually sent, the date that the fabricated steel was due on site ("DEL."), the date the steel actually arrived, the date the steel was to be lifted into position ("ERECT"), and finally the date that the steel was actually erected. This sequence was the heart of the steel construction process, and if examined, reveals a second major innovation of Starrett Brothers and Eken: fast-tracking.

Traditional design and construction was based on completing structural design before shop drawings were created by the fabricator, the shop drawings to be complete and reviewed before fabrication began, and fabrication to be complete or nearly complete before the start of steel erection on site. This sequence does not work well with time pressure, because each step depends on the completion of the step before. The system used on the Empire State, fairly new in 1930, but not original to the project, is what later became known as "fast-track" construction. The term covers many variations on the same idea—beginning construction before the design is complete.

Careful examination of the schedule in Fig. 1 shows that the design of the top tier (the eighty-fifth

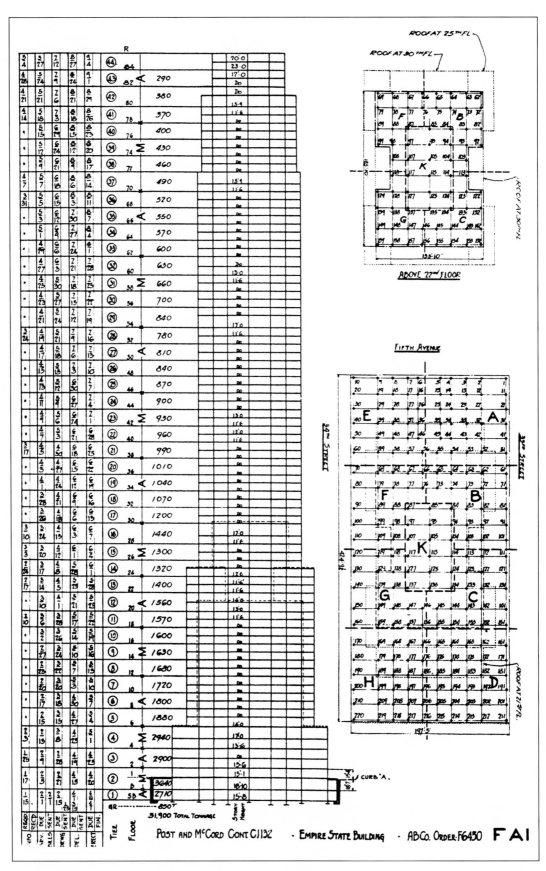

Fig. 1. Schedule for the structural steel for the Empire State Building, with dates of information and drawings required from the architects, mill orders, shop drawings, steel delivery, and steel erection. From Architectural Forum 52 (1930): 772.

floor and the main roof) was not required of Balcom's office until May 4, more than one month after steel erection of the first tier (the subbasement) was due to begin. Throughout the course of the project, Balcom's office was designing the steel less than one month before the mill orders were due. The shop drawings providing full detail for fabrication were being delivered less than six weeks before the steel was due to be delivered, and the steel was delivered from the fabricator to the erector's yard one week before it was due for erection. The last item resulted from limited on-site storage space, but the others were created solely by the owners' desire for speed.

The interlocking schedule of the steelwork was presented diagrammatically by Balcom, using the same dates as listed on the drawing (Fig. 2). Reading to the right on the chart shows time passing, reading up the chart shows the building rising. The first diagonal line represents the due dates for the design; the second, the mill order; the third, shop drawing completion; the fourth, delivery of steel to the site; and the fifth, the erection of the steel. The various activities on any given date can be examined by drawing a vertical line. For example, on May 1, the steel for the fourth and fifth floors had been delivered and was being erected, the steel for the sixth and seventh floors was awaiting erection, the steel for the eighth and ninth floors was due for delivery, and so on. Similarly, the various deadlines for any given floor can be determined by drawing a horizontal line.

This diagram clearly shows the amount of forethought required for fast-tracking to be successful. Each participant had several activities to perform. On any given day, steel for various tiers was in different stages of preparation, requiring attention from several of the consultants and construction companies. Fast-track speed required everyone to move together in step.

The use of fast-track construction for both the structural steel and some of the mechanical systems had the effect of locking the design in place early on. An irony of fast-tracking is that, by delaying portions of the design relative to the construction, there is less flexibility for changing those portions. Traditionally, the entire building existed on paper before any work began. Changes could be suggested by the owner, required by a government agency, or proposed by a contractor as a way to reduce cost. These changes can be made, on paper, at no cost except for the effort of the designers. In fast-track design, the lower portions of the building cannot be changed easily. If a change

at the upper floors requires redesign at the bottom, it necessitates reconstruction, and while this is not impossible, it is expensive and may obviate the advantages of fast tracking.

LESSONS FROM THE PAST

A building of the Empire State's status is not built every day. Paul Starrett called it the climax of his working life as well as the building that "expresses most completely and honestly the skyscraper idea."[11] Even allowing for his natural interest, his meaning is accurate: he was fortunate enough to work on one of the finest tall buildings ever built.

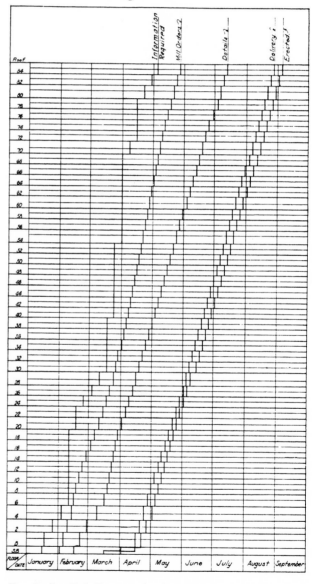

Fig. 2. Detailed Program for Manufacture and Erection of Structural Steel, Empire State Building, New York City. From The Economic Design of Office Buildings by R. H. Shreve, in Architectural Record 67 (1930): 346.

Most architects, engineers, and builders will not be as lucky as Starrett, but it is still possible to profit from a study of the construction of the Empire State. No one involved in the work was a lone genius; rather the group of architects, engineers, and contractors worked collectively to overcome the problems posed by a building and a building process that in many ways has not been surpassed.

The first and least subtle lesson is the benefit of cooperation. No single party could have ensured the completion of the building on time. Any one major party—the architects, the structural engineers, the mechanical engineers, the builders, the owners— could have blown the schedule. This group of people with similar but not identical goals managed to work together toward one carefully defined goal for twenty months, providing a reminder of the power of coordinated effort.

One of the important innovations that required full cooperation was fast-track construction. Fast-tracking, still an innovation in 1930, has since become common. Design may be complete before construction begins, but shop drawings never are. What was once an extraordinary measure to speed exceptional projects has become the. For anyone involved in the process to complain would be as futile as carping about any other increase in pace of modern life. The builders of the Empire State may bear some responsibility for bringing the fast track into the main stream, but the result of their work demonstrated that this technique is capable of being used intelligently and producing good results.

An important lesson in the pursuit of speed was to disconnect different portions of the work as much as possible. Trades move at different speeds, have special requirements, and may view the same detail in entirely different ways. By eliminating as much of the contact between trades as was possible, the builders reduced the risk of cascading delays. While not explicitly stated as a goal, various portions of the work show the idea in action: the curtain wall support detail removed the dependence of the steel fabricator and erector on masonry information; concrete batching on site freed the mixers from Manhattan's traffic conditions; and the coordinated use of materials hoists, passenger elevators, and the industrial railroad system controlled the chaotic movement through the site. These examples are specific to the Empire State, but the general lesson was learned by the building community and helped spur the growth of construction management firms, which advertised, among other benefits, their ability to organize and control subcontractors.

The final lesson includes all the others: the benefits of planning. From the moment that the group of designers and builders assembled, its members were working simultaneously on immediate deadlines and on items that would be required a few months ahead. Planning for all of the deadlines is a necessary element in fast-tracking, in the methodical organization of the trades, and ultimately in the ability of the different parties to cooperate. If the most lasting statistics of the Empire State are based on speed, their basis is careful planning. This may be a sober way to look at a romantic building, but it is in the end the most fitting tribute to its builders.

NOTES

1. William Starrett, *Skyscrapers and the Men Who Build Them* (New York: Charles Scribner's Sons, 1928), 178.

2. J. Webster Boyes, Starrett Brothers and Eken, Inc., "Compression of Steel: Empire State Building," n.d., unpublished.

3. R. H. Shreve, "The Empire State Building, II: The Window-Spandrel-Wall Detail and its Relation to Building Progress," *Architectural Forum* (July 1930): 99–105.

4. H. L. Richardson, "The Empire State Building, V: Electrical Equipment,"*Architectural Forum* (November 1930): 639–644.

5. "The Building of a Skyscraper," reprinted from the *New York Globe*, January 26, 1909, in *Skyscraper-Building,*

Theodore Starrett, New York, 1907, no publisher.

6. J. L. Edwards, "The Empire State Building, III: The Structural Frame," *Architectural Forum* (August 1930): 241–246.

7. "Planning and Control Permit Erection of 85 Stories of Steel in Six Months," *Engineering News-Record* (August 21, 1930).

8. Paul Starrett, *Changing the Skyline: An Autobiography* (New York: McGraw-Hill, 1938), 295.

9. "Twentieth Century Building Construction", reprinted from the *New York Herald*, January 2, 1907, reprinted in *Skyscraper-Building*.

10. P. Starrett, 290.

11. P. Starrett, *Changing the Skyline*, 284.

BUILDING
THE
EMPIRE
STATE

Corner of 5th Ave. and 34th Street.
Astoria Section.

("C" 9/27/29)

View at 5th Avenue and 34th Street.

Despite its late-Victorian architecture and the massive appearance of its exterior masonry walls, the Astoria section of the Waldorf-Astoria Hotel, completed in 1897, was a steel-frame building. In the two months elapsed between the photos, the exterior skin and interior partitions were removed, leaving only the steel frame and terra-cotta tile floors. Older demolition methods designed to demolish heavy masonry bearing walls—basically pounding the material until it collapsed—were used on the masonry portions of the building, then were followed by the more modern demolition technique of using torches to burn the steel apart. ("F" 11/27/29)

NOTES ON CONSTRUCTION OF EMPIRE STATE BUILDING

WRECKING THE WALDORF ASTORIA HOTEL

(An empty hotel)

A contemporary poet described in poignant verse the air of lonesomeness and sadness surrounding a "house with nobody in it". Whenever he passed it standing alone in solitude he always felt it deserved a better fate than desertion because it had been a "home that had sheltered life".

On September 23, 1929, a group of five men visited the Waldorf Astoria Hotel (bounded by 5th Ave., Astor Court, 34th and 33d Sts.) in New York City and made a preliminary survey with the idea of getting the demolition work started immediately. The hotel had been unoccupied for about six months and it would take the poet referred to above to describe the air of utter solitude and desolation within the walls of the grand hostelry - in its day one of the finest hotels in the world.

Our purpose, however, is not to describe the life and beauty of its living days but is the more prosaic one of showing the facts and figures of how destruction was completely accomplished, down to the very last stone buried below the old machinery foundations, on March 12, 1930 - less than five months later.

The total reduction of these buildings resulted in 24,321 loads of material, principally debris which was dumped from scows, 20 miles out at sea.

SOUVENIR HUNTERS

Americans are very often accused of being devoid of sentiment, but for the benefit of our critics it might be well to state that more than a thousand written requests were received from practically every State in the Union and a few requests came from abroad for souvenirs of the hotel before the work of demolition was completed.

All the furnishings had been sold at auction some months before, but many people wrote in for fixtures and various items of practical nature that could be used in connection with their own homes.

To select just a few of these requests at random. A man from Keokuk, Iowa, requests the iron railing fence along the 5th Ave. side of the building. A woman in Connecticut wants a balcony railing for her country house. A man from Maine wants a flagpole. A request from Miller River, State of Washington, is for some stained glass windows. Over a thousand doors were shipped to Florida to be used in a new institutional building. Numerous requests were received for fireplaces, pieces of marble, bricks and stone and lighting fixtures. One man and his wife were made very happy by being able to secure the key to the room they had occupied many years before while on their honeymoon.

All of the mural paintings, including the large painting from the ceiling of the Grand Ballroom, were salvaged with some of the interior woodwork for the Waldorf Astoria Corporation for possible future use in the new Waldorf Astoria Hotel now being constructed on the corner of Lexington Avenue and 49th Street.

MATERIAL SALVAGED

Lighting fixtures and articles of a portable nature, which were generally sold to individuals at the building during the demolition period could be grouped as follows:

Electrical Fixtures	Railings and Grilles	Gates
Plumbing Fixtures	Brass Mouldings	Fire Backs
Glass and Mirrors	Revolving Doors	Andirons
Radiators	Statues	Lockers
Marble	Elevator Doors	Mail Chutes
Wood Doors	Mural Paintings	
Frame Mantlepieces	Brass Railing Brackets	
Woodwork Carvings	Cast Iron Figures	
Marble Mantlepieces	Terra Cotta Railings	
Door Checks	Safes	
Hardware	Bronze Store Fronts	

The bulk material items sold and trucked away from the site, consisted of the following:

    14,615 tons structural steel and miscellaneous scrap iron
        36 tons scrap copper
         8 tons of brass, lead and zinc

ENGINE ROOM EQUIPMENT

All of the plant and equipment in the basement were sold as a unit to a dealer who had to remove same.

This equipment included all the machinery of the light, heat, ventilation, power, refrigeration and plumbing plants and some idea of the volume of this material can be gained from the various units listed below:-

7 Babcock Wilcox boilers
4 Generators - electric plant - 120 volt, 200 K.W. direct connected to Ed. P. Allis Corlis valve engines.
2 Generators - electric plant - 120 volt, 100 K.W. direct connected to Ed. P. Allis Corlis valve engines.
1 Ice machine - 40 tons capacity - including York two-stage ammonia compressor uniflow engine.
2 Ice machines - rebuilt De La Vergne ammonia compressors - 20 tons capacity - with Corlis engines.
2 Gurney elevators - capacity 2500 lbs., speed 400 ft. per min. together with control boards - drum type
8 Motors in sub-basement.
5 Motors in first basement
4 Motor generators in sub-basement.
2 Blake-Knowles single stage 12" x 20" x 24" compressors in sub-basement.
12 Worthington high pressure pumps (2 in electric plant pit).
2 Sump Pumps
4 Fuel oil pumps - size $7\frac{1}{2}$ x $4\frac{1}{2}$ x 10.
2 Worthington boiler feed pumps.
3 Worthington brine pumps.
1 Worthington drip pump, size $7\frac{1}{2}$ x $4\frac{1}{2}$ x 6.
1 Single stage air pump.
2 Laidlaw-Dun Gordon compressors.
2 Blaisdell vacuum compressors.
2 Sprague electric dumbwaiters in sub-basement.
1 150 gallon Ruud Automatic gas heater (hot water) in Astor Court Bldg.

All piping generally in both basements was included in this contract. Also, all valves and piping used for connecting up the machinery units.

The sub-contractor started removal of the above material on Nov.1, 1929 and completed his contract on Feb.5, 1930.

All of this material was removed during the progress of the wrecking generally in such a manner as not to interfere with the work of the general contractor, who was doing the actual wrecking work at the same time. This work of removing the machinery was done on week days between 8:00 A.M. and 5:00 P.M. and on Saturdays between 8:00 A.M. and noon.

SALVAGE OF FOUR A.B.SEE ELEVATORS

Four complete A.B.See passenger elevators, which had been installed in hotel for about five years prior to start of demolition work, were salvaged and reinstalled for temporary use during construction period of Empire State Building.

Corner of 5th Avenue and 33rd Street.
Waldorf Section.

The Waldorf section of the Waldorf-Astoria, completed in 1892, only five years before the Astoria, used a previous generation of structure: cast-iron columns, masonry bearing walls, and wrought-iron beams. In this case, the heavy, ornate masonry shown in the photograph is bearing structure and therefore had to be demolished with more care than the non-bearing walls of the Astoria section. ("A" 9/27/29)

View looking towards Astor Court Building
with large chimney in foreground.

The Astor Court Building was a steel-frame structure similar to the Astoria, and, reflecting its status as the last portion of the Waldorf-Astoria built, had the least ornamentation on its exterior non-bearing walls. ("B" 9/27/29)

FOUR BUILDINGS COMPRISED COMPLETE UNIT
TO BE WRECKED

Size of buildings:

The Waldorf Hotel Section - which was the original Waldorf Hotel, completed in 1892, was a twelve-story building of sandstone exterior, with terra cotta floor arch and terra cotta fireproof construction throughout . It was of semi-wall bearing type of construction with cast iron columns and wrought iron floor beams and girders.

The dimensions of the building were 100 ft. in width on 5th Ave., 250 ft., in depth on West 33d St. with an average height of 12 stories, totaling 164 ft.

It contained 4,100,000 cubic feet capacity from street level to roof .

The Waldorf Annex - was a four-story annex to the Waldorf Hotel Building, adjoining same on 33d St. side with the other end at Astor Court. This building was completed in 1897. It was of steel frame construction with sandstone exterior with terra cotta floor arches and terra cotta fireproofing throughout.

The dimensions were 100 ft. in width, 85 ft. in depth, with a four-story height of 78 ft. 3 inches.

It contained 665,000 cubic feet capacity from street level to roof.

The Astoria Section - of the hotel was completed in 1897. It adjoined the Waldorf Section with a frontage of approximately 100 ft. on 5th Ave. and a depth of 335 ft. on West 34th St. The sixteen-story height of this building was 216 ft.

It contained 7,245,000 cubic feet capacity from street level to roof.

The Astor Court Building - was an eight-story limestone structure used as an office building with a steel frame, terra cotta arches and terra cotta fireproofing throughout. It faced Astor Court and extended from 33d St. to 34th St. The street known as Astor Court, which was 50 ft. wide, separated the Astor Court Building from the Waldorf Astoria Hotel Building.

The dimensions were 200 ft. wide by 40 ft. deep, with an eight story height of 112 ft. 5 inches, and contained 900,000 cubic feet capacity from street level to roof.

The two basements of the hotel property extended under Astor Court and the Astor Court Building to the west lot property line.

View at 5th Avenue and 33rd Street.

Because the bearing walls of the Waldorf acted in concert with the iron frame to keep the building stable, the masonry could not be demolished first. In this photograph, the Waldorf has been reduced to roughly half its original height, but the work is proceeding simultaneously across the topmost remaining floor, rather than by material type. The Astoria (in the background) has been stripped of all its masonry, and, at the upper floors, of its terra-cotta floors. ("E" 11/27/29)

View towards Astor Court and 34th Street. Astor Court Building in foreground.

The Astor Court building has been reduced to a bare steel frame at its uppermost floors, while the exterior masonry removal is in progress at its base. ("D" 11/27/29)

TIME INVOLVED IN DEMOLITION WORK
BUILDINGS WRECKED TO SIDEWALK LEVEL

Actual demolition work on the group of buildings started on Sept. 24, 1929 and all the masonery and steel was completely demolished to sidewalk level on Feb. 3, 1930.

The masonry was completely wrecked to sidewalk level on Jan. 13, 1930. Started Sept. 24, 1929, finished Jan. 13, 1930 meant approximately 86 working days to accomplish this task, figuring 4 hours work on each Saturday.

The steel structure was completely wrecked to sidewalk level on Feb. 3, 1930. This work was started on Oct.4, 1929 and finished Feb. 3, 1930 (no Saturday work included) or in approximately 87 working days.

MATERIAL CONTAINED IN SUPERSTRUCTURE

The material disposed of from buildings down to sidewalk level consisted of 16,508 loads of debris, each load having a capacity of 5-1/2 cu. yds. place measurement, or a total of 90,794 cu. yds.

The steel down to sidewalk level consisted of 12,097 tons.

Section of cantilever truss over Grand Ballroom. Astoria section.

This demolition photograph shows many of the distinguishing characteristics of steel frame construction of 1897. These techniques were a generation old and had been modified or replaced by the time the Empire State was designed. All of the large steel members visible—the diagonal truss strut, the columns, and the large girders—are built up of small angles, channels, and plates riveted together. The connection within the truss—from the top of the vertical hanger in the center of the photograph to the diagonal strut—is a large round pin, similar to those used in bridge construction. The floors were all terra-cotta arches, removed first because they are so easily broken. ("G" 1/2/30)

METHOD OF STRUCTURAL STEEL DEMOLITION:

All of the structural steel in the Waldorf-Astoria Hotel and Astor Court Buildings was removed by burning with oxy-acetylene torches. This steel was lowered to the street with the aid of one 25 ton steel derrick and two 15-ton steel derricks, which were first set up on the roof of the Astoria Section - one 7½ ton steel derrick on the roof of the Waldorf Section - one 10 ton steel derrick on the roof of the Waldorf Annex, and one 5 ton Dennis derrick on the roof of the Astor Court Building.

Our records show that 17 oxy-acetylene torches were used during the course of the work - also to supply fuel for these torches -
802,000 cubic feet of oxygen
195,000   "   " acetylene gas were used.

METHOD OF DEMOLISHING SIDE WALLS AND FLOORS:

The brick and sandstone masonry of the exterior walls were drilled with 7/8 inch hollow drill steel in Ingersoll-Rand Pneumatic Rotary Jackhammers, the holes afterwards plugged and feathered, and pieces of masonry wedged out and dropped in small sections to the floor inside the buildings.

The floor arches, which were of terra cotta construction, were broken down by using Ingersoll-Rand Concrete Breakers, which were equipped with a special shoe shaped steel to break the terra cotta floor arch down to the floor below.

All debris was dumped into wooden chutes located inside the building, extending from the floor on which the wrecking was being done down through to the main floor.

The debris was loaded from these chute hoppers on main floor into Mack 5-ton trucks, equipped with special 24 inch sideboards, from whence it was taken to scows at East River and 32nd St. Extra large pieces of masonry debris, which could not be dumped into scow without fear of breaking the hatches on same, had to be sent to the land dump at Maspeth , L.I. Scrap wood and tin also had to be sent to the land dump.

DISPOSAL OF DEBRIS, ETC:

Loading of the trucks with debris was accomplished almost entirely within the building on the main floor. The exception was the loading of scrap wood, which was piled on sidewalk bridge and then loaded into the trucks in the street directly below the bridge.

ONE STORY DEMOLISHING AT A TIME:

In order to carry on the work of demolition of all masonry with a maximum of safety for the workmen, it was necessary to wreck only one story at a time.

EQUIPMENT:

The air for the pneumatic drills and paving breakers was supplied by 2-Stage Electric Ingersoll-Rand Compressors, capable of supplying air for 80 Jackhammers.

These compressors were erected on 34th St. sidewalk, projecting 3 ft. over curb into the street.

FORCE ACCOUNT:

When demolition work on the superstructure reached its peak on Nov.22,1929, a force of 719 men was employed.

Cantilever truss over Grand Ballroom. Astoria Section.

Removal of one of the largest individual pieces of structure in the Waldorf-Astoria, the truss over the ballroom. The older style of steel framing, using small pieces of steel riveted together to form beams and columns, is clearly visible. ("H" 1/2/30)

AIR LINES:

Old steam risers of the existing buildings were used for extending compressed air lines to upper floors where hammers were working.

OUTRIGGER PROTECTION:

A protection scaffold extending 12 feet from the face of the building with a 3 feet baffle on the end was constructed and placed all around the building to protect the men working on the walls and pedestrains in the streets by preventing debris from falling.

This scaffold was removed and reconstructed several times during the downward course of the demolition work.

DUST:

On account of the close proximty of several department stores with their merchandise on display, a special effort was made to protect the wares and also the shopper and general public by trying to minimize the circulation of dust during the wrecking period. By the extensive use of water in wetting down the debris, and also by loading trucks almost entirely inside the building, we succeeded in causing very little annoyance to our neighbors and to pedestrains.

WRECKING AND REMOVING OLD WALLS AND FOUNDATIONS BELOW STREET LEVEL:

The work of demolishing and removing the old walls and foundations, including the structural steel contained below the street level, was started on January 14th, 1930 and completely finished on March 12th, 1930 (Saturdays included), or in approximately 50 working days of two shifts each day.

BLASTING:

All of the massive inside walls and machinery foundations had to be drilled and blasted with dynamite.

OUTSIDE FOUNDATION WALLS:

All of the building line foundation walls were cut away from steel beams supporting sidewalks and pushed back with the aid of 60 ton screw jacks into the excavation, where sections were blasted into smaller pieces, suitable for loading on trucks.

EQUIPMENT USED:

The debris from old foundations was removed in 5-ton Mack trucks which used ramps as runways to and from the excavation.

A list of the large equipment items employed during this period will give an idea of the speed which had to be employed to prepare the way for setting grillage beams on March 20th, 1930, on the new concrete column pier footings, in order to receive the first steel columns which were set on April 8th.

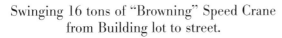

Demolition stage on Jan. 9th 1930.
View at 33rd Street and 5th Avenue.

As demolition neared completion, the last remaining structure above sidewalk grade is a portion of the steel frame of the Astor Court building. The demolition continued below grade, as the basement floors and columns had to be removed down to bedrock in order to provide proper bearing for the footings below the Empire State columns. ("J" 1/9/30)

Swinging 16 tons of "Browning" Speed Crane
from Building lot to street.

The Browning crane was used for heavy work below grade during the demolition and the early portions of the new construction. Once the new foundations were complete, the crane was no longer needed, and was lifted out of the cellar pit by one of the larger cranes that would shortly be used for steel erection. (#32 4/2/30)

PARTIAL LIST OF EQUIPMENT

2-Large 2-stage Ingersoll Rand Electric Compressors 1245 cu.ft.per min.ea.
1-One-stage Ingersoll Rand Electric Compressor
2-8x10 Gasoline Air Compressors
20-Ingersoll Rand Pneumatic Paving Breaker Machines
80- "   "   "   Jack Hammers
2- X71 Quarry Bar Drilling Machines
22- Cu.Yd. Steel Scale Boxes
2-Ingersoll Rand Oil Burning Forges
2- "   "   Drill Sharpening Machines
2-Blacksmith Shop Equipment Units
2-Dynamite Outfits
4-Thow Gasoline Shovels
1-Koering Gasoline Shovel
1-Brouning Crane
2-Moore Speed Cranes
2-Ten ton Stiff Leg Derricks.

Force Account:

A copy of the daily job diary for March 11th, when this work of wrecking old walls and foundations was at its peak, shows that 664 men were employed on that date.

Quantities Excavated:

From the old walls and foundations of the Hotel and Astor Court buildings 6,301 loads of debris were removed, each load containing about 3½ yds. place measurement, or 22,000 cubic yards.

The structural steel and miscellaneous scrap iron from old walls and foundations totalled 2518 tons.

SUMMARY OF LOADS OF MATERIAL REMOVED FROM WRECKED BUILDINGS ABOVE SIDEWALK LEVEL AND OLD WALLS AND OLD FOUNDATIONS BELOW SIDEWALK

	Loads Removed from Wrecked Buildings Above Sidewalks:	Loads removed from Old Walls and Foundations:
Debris	15,738 Loads	6,246 Loads
Firewood	770 "	56 "
Structural Steel and Misc.Scrap iron	1,184 "	298 "
Scrap copper	26 "	--
" brass	3 "	--
" lead	1 Load	--
	17,722 Loads	6,599 Loads

A Grand Total of 24,321 Loads of Material represents the final quantity wrecked from the old buildings.

Excavation nearly complete.

The Empire State is the third building to occupy most of its site. The hotel buildings had replaced small houses that were the first buildings constructed on the vacant land. As a result, excavation meant removing not only earth and rock, but also the remnants of old masonry and concrete foundations. This is a typical condition in Manhattan, which makes excavation slower and potentially more dangerous than in more rural settings. (#21 3/21/30)

First Grillages set on piers.

Manhattan bedrock is mostly granite and schist and is capable of supporting extremely high loads, but its elevation varies widely. At this site, it ranged to seventy feet below grade, requiring concrete piers to transmit the loads from the base of the steel columns down to bedrock. The tops of these piers were reinforced with grillages—mats of steel beams set at right angles, which spread the concentrated load from the column base across the width of the pier. (#29 4/1/30)

E M P I R E S T A T E B U I L D I N G

CONSTRUCTION WORK STARTS

General Cellar and Trench Excavation:

The general excavation started on January 22, 1930, and was carried on concurrently with wrecking of the old walls and foundations.

This work was completely finished on March 17, 1930

The material excavated consisted of: 9,000 cu.yds. of earth
                                     17,398 "   "   " rock

The sub-basement floor for new building is approximately five (5) feet below the old sub-basement floor level of hotel building.

Pier Hole Excavation:

The pier hole excavation started on February 12,1930, and first pier holes passed hard rock bottom test by City Inspector and were filled with concrete on February 24, 1930.

The pier holes were completely excavated on March 29,1930

The material excavated from pier holes consisted of 463 cubic yards of earth and 4,992 cubic yards of rock.

The rock in many of the pier holes in the tower section was soft and in some pier holes it was required to go from 30 to 40 ft. below sub-basement floor elevation to strike the hard rock necessary to pass test required before concrete could be poured into the holes.

Concrete Footings for Steel Columns:

The work of pouring the concrete column footings took place immediately after pier holes passed the necessary hard rock tests, and the total of 210 concrete piers were completely finished by March 29,1930.

The concrete yardage poured into 210 piers totalled 3,744 cubic yards.

A chart, showing the make-up of Job Organization follows :-

EMPIRE STATE BLDG
JOB ORGANIZATION — AT PEAK

STARRETT BROTHERS and EKEN
INCORPORATED.

SUPERINTENDENT
J.W. BOWSER

PROJECT MANAGER
H.J. STELLMANN
ASS'T PROJECT MGR
T.F. GUNN
STENOGRAPHER
R. KING

ENGINEERING
N. EASTWOOD

CONSTRUCTION DIVISION
J. CARL
ASS'T SUP'T

ACCOUNTING DIVISION
H. LONG
ACCOUNTANT
C. HEBLING
STENOGRAPHER

PRODUCTION AND COST
DISTRIBUTION ENGINEER
J.W. CARLSON
STENOGRAPHER

PRODUCTION
ENGINEER
J.W. DAVIS Jr.

— Engineering inspectors —
INSPECTOR OF STEEL & ENGINEERING
INSPECTOR OF ELEVATOR OR CONSTRUCTION
INSPECTOR OF GEN'L MATERIAL — J. HARDING
INSPECTOR OF ELECTRICAL MATERIAL
INSPECTOR OF CAULKING — J. STACY
INSPECTOR OF PLUMBING, HEATING AIR — F. HELLMANN
INSPECTOR OF SMALL METAL, TERRAZZO, CEMENT FLOORS, MARBLE — R. GRIFFITHS
CIVIL ENG'R GRADES, MEASUREMENTS, LAYOUTS — J.W. BOYES, J. KISSEL
TEMPORARY LIGHT & POWER — E.O. McGANAHAY
MAIN OFFICE ESTIMATOR & ENGINEER ON STONE AND MARBLE — P.J. HYNES

— Construction Division —
FOREMAN OF PIPEFITTERS — J. McLEER
FOREMEN OF LATHERS — W. COLLINS
WATCHMEN AND FIRE PATROL — J. SCULLY
STOREKEEPERS — T. THOMAS
FOREMAN OF SMALL CARPENTERS — P. O'BRIEN
FOREMAN OF TRAFFIC — W. WHALEN
MASTER MECHANIC — C. VAN BRUNT
FOREMAN OF GENERAL LABOR — M. MARHULOFF
FOREMAN OF STONEWORK — J. MUIR
FOREMAN OF CONCRETE — J. RICCARDI
FOREMAN CARPENTER BACK WORK — W. BLAIS
FOREMAN OF MASONRY — E. JUDD

— Accounting Division —
MONTHLY COST STATEMENTS — A. HARGRAFT
PURCHASING AGENT — W.T. BENNETT, F. MOLLOY ASS'T
RECEIVING, FILING AND DISTRIBUTING DRAWINGS — R. MARGADONNA
EXPEDITING — J. STEEN, J. ROBERTS
CONTRACT CHANGES AND ESTIMATING — G. DRIES ASS'T PROJECT MGR
TIMECHECKING — L. LOTTIER HEAD CHECKER, 9 CHECKERS
RECEIVING MATERIALS — J.M. DERMOTT MAT'L CLERK, 4 ASSISTANTS
DAILY COST COMPILATION — A. LATIMER
TIMEKEEPING AND PAY ROLLS — R. VELSEY TIMEKEEPER, 2 CLERKS
BILL CLERK — W. GRANBERRY
COST & RECORDS CLERK — T. O'HAGAN

— Production —
FIELD HOSPITAL — DR. A. WOLFF, MISS GACH RN
MESSENGER — H. LIESKE
TELEPHONE OPERATOR — J. LEICHTMAN
FIELD COST DISTRIBUTION — J.F. McKENNA, 3 CLERKS

JOB ORGANIZATION

The formidable task of supervising the construction of a building that is to be at once the largest and tallest building in the world - a building that has to be finished within the space of one year from start of setting the steel, requires first of all a highly trained organization on the part of the Builders. It must contain a personnel of individual specialists who can take charge and carry through a definite program that requires the closest kind of co-ordination between the branches of work being done by the Builders and about forty subcontractors, practically all of whom are working on the building at the same time.

Directly in charge of all the work is the Job Superintendent. On an operation of this magnitude, a man is required with a forceful and aggressive personality, tempered with the qualities of tact and infinite patience. Of course, it is understood he must possess a thorough knowledge of building construction. The main departments under his supervision are as follows:

Job Runner's Department:

The title "Job Runner", which has come into common usage, is one that seems wholly inappropriate for the class of work under the control of that individual. Under his direction a liaison is established between Owners, Architects, Job Organization and all subcontractors. This involves the receiving, filing and distributing of all plans and shop drawings, interpreting of plans for job organization and subcontractors, preparation of contracts, change orders and estimating for tenant changes and variations from original plans, expediting material and mill and shop inspection.

Construction Department:

This branch is in charge of all construction work, such as masonry, stone, concrete, carpentry and has direct supervision of all the work installed by subcontractors. The Civil and Mechanical Engineering departments, and all the various field inspection units which have direct inspection control of the mechanical and architectural construction work, are also a part of the Construction Department.

All the day and night watchmen and the fire patrol forces employed on the building are also under this Department.

Accounting Division:

Under this division are the auditing and bookkeeping, timekeeping and payroll departments; departments for purchasing and receiving of materials, and with the aid of the Construction Department, the Production and Costs department survey the work put in place each day and work out the analysis of daily labor cost that enables a daily unit labor cost to be set up against each operation of importance. This daily labor unit cost is the barometer which enables the Superintendent to ascertain if the work of each particular class is being done at a loss or gain as compared with the unit allowed in the preliminary cost estimate, and is of supreme importance in assisting him to keep his labor forces under economical control.

A very close supervision exists also between the Superintendent and the Purchasing Department. All requisitions for purchase of materials and equipment have to clear through the Superintendent for approval before same can be purchased, thereby restricting items purchased to those

Sidewalk Bridge Bungalows (5th Avenue)

All construction sites require temporary buildings to house the general contractors' offices, often called "shanties" or "bungalows." A striking feature of the Empire State bungalows is their number and careful construction. On a project where logistics was of paramount importance, the general contractor made certain that adequate offices were provided. Cramped or haphazard temporary space would be inefficient and might have slowed the project. (#20 3/18/30)

Office towards switchboard
Bungalow #1.

The interior of the temporary office, while compact, is not particularly different from any other engineering office of the era. (#167 6/21/30)

actually needed.

A chart, showing the make-up of Job Organization follows:-

<u>Temporary Office for Construction Force:</u>

Immediately after the sidewalk bridge was constructed, temporary offices were built for the Builder on Fifth Avenue sidewalk bridge, with an additional office building extending on the 33d St. side, west of 5th Ave.

These buildings furnished offices for the Builders, for Owner's organization, for Field Hospital and for Inspector of the Metropolitan Life Insurance Company, until such time as sidewalk bridge had to be demolished and space found in the new building about one year after their construction.

The offices for all the subcontractors were constructed within the building of a corrugated metal exterior of 26-gauge and were all confined to the third floor. To lessen the fire hazard, all temporary shacks placed within the building were constructed with this 26-gauge corrugated metal exterior.

<u>System of Timekeeping:</u>

The method used by the Builders, in hiring, laying off and checking the men in the field is substantially the same system used by the various subcontractors. The hiring of men for the different trades is done by the respective trade foreman. All hiring is done before 8 A.M. on the main floor in the direct vicinity of the timekeeper's office. Each man hired, is given a hiring ticket, upon which is written his name, class, rate of pay and time and date hired. He presents this ticket to the timekeeper's office where a personnel card is filled in with his name, age, home address, and a notation if he is single or married - and the number of children in the latter case. There is also a record of earnings kept upon his personnel card for income tax record.

At the timekeeper's office he is assigned a number and given a small brass disc bearing the same number. The brass check is given to him each morning at the time office when he reports for work and he presents it at the time office when he finishes work each day.

During the day, field time checkers visit every man on the building; once in the morning and once in the afternoon and ask him to show his brass check. This gives four checks each day on every man; when he reports for work at the time office, during the forenoon, during the afternoon and when he turns in his check each night. On Friday morning (pay day) he receives an aluminum check bearing his number, in addition to his regular brass check. He presents the aluminum check to paymaster when he receives his pay.

<u>Payroll Division:</u>

The information showing the actual number of hours each individual worked each day is forwarded to the Payroll Division where it is posted on the payroll.

Some idea of the size of the weekly payroll involved, can be gained by noting the payroll for the week ending September 20th, 1930 - when, for 1928 men employed by the General Contractor, the payroll amounted to $141,466.85. Considering the various subcontractors had 1511 men in addition to the above on their payrolls for the same week, it is safe to estimate the combined total payroll for the week as approximately $250,000.00 .

Armored Service men paying in field.

Weekly wages were paid on site. At peak activity in the summer of 1930, the payroll was about $250,000 a week, making the armored guards necessary. (#285 9/26/30)

Paying the Men in the Field:

When the payroll has been duly audited, a check for the total amount is drawn and this check, together with change list, and the required number of empty pay envelopes – each having written upon it the number and name of the workman and the amount he is to receive – are all turned over to the Armored Service Corporation. They fill the envelopes at the bank and arrive at the building each Friday at 8 A.M. with the money in an armored car and the required number of armed guards, and in company with paymasters of the General Contractor visit each man throughout the building and pay him his envelope after he has presented an aluminum check, bearing his number, and told his name. Timecheckers for the Builder are always available if any further identification of any man is required.

The aluminum check mentioned above is handed out by timekeeper each Friday morning, in addition to regular brass check when man reports at time office at start of day's work.

The payroll week ends at 5 P.M. on Wednesday. Payrolls are completely checked and audited on Wednesday night. Thursday is devoted by the Armored Service Corporation to filling envelopes. Friday, the men are paid on the job. Saturday, is regarded as a holiday. A five-day week has prevailed on the job.

System of Checking in Field for Labor Cost Distribution:

Entirely independent of the field time checking force is a field labor cost distribution organization which checks each man at least four times a day in the field in relation to the kind of work he is doing. A summary is made for each trade or class on foremen's daily reports (compiled by this department), which show on one side the number of the individual man checked with the total hours each man worked for the day. To insure correct totals, a reconciliation is made with the time department check. On the back of each foreman's daily report sheet a distribution is made of the various activities under the different accounting sub-division symbols, which insures that each man's time is charged as accurately as possible to the work performed.

This method takes away from the foreman the clerical work involved in preparing daily reports and also removes the temptation of favoring accounts upon which a daily unit cost is worked out at the expense of those general condition accounts upon which no daily cost unit is compiled.

A digest of the activities of the men as obtained by the distribution checkers, is incorporated in the daily job diary, which gives a complete record of the day's activities.

Production Department:

A survey is made each day of the various quantities put in place on all those accounts upon which a daily cost unit is worked out. Once each week a physical inventory is taken of the different kinds of material on hand and this inventory acts as a check against quantities surveyed in place in the field.

The division of the various quantities placed into the cost of labor, results in the daily cost unit, which enables the Superintendent to ascertain if he is running above or below the unit allowed in his preliminary cost estimate.

Workmen's Restaurant - 3rd floor.

Temporary lunch counters within a construction site were nearly unique in 1930 and still are. Construction companies are not obligated to provide food service, and most do not, but the scale of the Empire State project presented a problem. Rather than having large numbers of workers using the elevators twice each lunch hour, several food concessions were provided, so men stayed closer to their work. (#190 7/9/30)

The Feeding Problem:

Before granting a concession for resturant privileges on the building, the thought in mind was to consult some of the better class resturant owners in the immediate vicinity and find one who in point of integrity, plant and equipment could take care of the flexible demands of a rapidly growing construction organization - one that would reach its peak in a total of 3500 men.

A high class resturant operator, with three resturants in the vicinity was told he could have the privilege for a very nominal sum per month (enough to pay for light and power), if he would agree to have the Builders construct for him, at resturant owner's expense, five lunch stands as the progress of the work required them. These lunch stands were built, when needed, on the 3d floor, 9th floor and 24th floor, 47th floor and 64th floor, and were completely equipeed by the resturant owner and remained in these locations throughout the life of the job.

It was further agreed that he would serve food of the finest quality the same as in his regular resturant, but at slightly reduced rates. In this way, good food at economical prices was purchased by the men and they were completely satisfied throughout the course of the work.

Innumerable inquiries were made by those anxious to secure this valuable concession, but the thought of the General Contractors and the Owners in the matter was that no high price for a rental privilege should be taken from some concessionaire who would have to make his profits by serving inferior food, or high priced food to the men.

The result of the arrangement as worked out, was that the resturant man made a fair profit, the men bought food at cheaper prices than same could be purchased outside the building, and the very vexing problem of getting 3500 men in and out of the building during the lunch hour with limited elevator service was satisfactorily solved. Not more than 15% of the men left the building during the lunch hour period.

Sandwiches of all kinds, hot coffee, milk, near beer, soft drinks, ice cream, candies and cigarettes and tobacco were sold. Hot and cold dishes of food were served on pressed paper plates, or in containers, such as chicken salad, beef stew, beefsteak pie, frankfurters and sauerkraut - and these dishes, which were substantial, could be taken away and eaten in picnic lunch style and became very popular with the men.

Many of the men who brought their own lunches, found that the food was made more palatable by securing a container of hot coffee or milk, or some of the soft drink beverages sold at the lunch stands.

During the life of the entire job not one complaint was received concerning the quality or price of the food served. This is a remarkable record, in view of the fact that the commissary department on every construction operation is generally the source of prolific complaints, and in many cases without justification. When groups of people congregate, whether it be on a construction job, or in the world's finest hotel, a criticism of food seems to be always entirely in order. It is a common trait in human nature.

This service was conducted by James P. Sullivan of Lord's Chain of resturants - main headquarters, 33 West 33d St., N.Y.City.

Foremen and Engineers' Shanty - 2nd floor.

The Foremen and Engineers' Shanty was the office of the people directly in charge of the work. The engineers referred to in the text are operating engineers—the people who operated the heavy machinery—not design engineers. (#178 7/2/40)

Timekeeper's Shanty - 1st floor.

The Timekeeper's Shanty, located on the first floor of the building, was a key location for controlling the flow of people through the site. The worker's timecards and timeclock were here (and are visible through the open door). The sign on the side of the shanty is instructive: anyone hoping to get work by slipping onto the site with the workers and talking to a foreman was going to be disappointed, by policy. (#191 7/9/30)

DAILY JOB ACTIVITY

Perhaps, the best way to get a cross section of the varied activities of the many men employed on a building operation of this size is to glance at the job diary.

Each day a diary is compiled, which corresponds to the log of a ship. This diary is required to give a record of the number of men employed and a digest of the activities of the various trades and groups.

Our records show that Thursday, August 14th, 1930, was the day upon which the greatest number of men were employed - namely, 3,439 of whom 1928 were working for the Builders and 1511 for the various sub-contractors. But let the diary for that day tell its own story. It is a cross section of the job's activity at its busiest period.

STARRETT BROTHERS and EKEN
Incorporated

Building: Empire State   Date: Thursday, August 14, 1930

Location: 5th Ave., W. 33d & W.34th Sts.   Weather: Fair

Architect: Shreve, Lamb & Harmon   Temperature 68° 8 AM 72° 2 PM

Superintendent: John W. Bowser

DAILY CONSTRUCTION REPORT

No. Men   Remarks:

Starrett Brothers and Eken, Incorporated

Supervising Overhead:

1	Superintendent
1	Asst. Superintendent
1	Job Runner
2	Asst. Job Runners
1	Accountant
1	Purchasing Agent
1	Engineer
1	Asst. to Supt.
4	Stenographers
1	Plan Clerk
1	Telephone Operator
1	Office Boy
16	

Operating Overhead:

1	Asst. Superintendent
1	Civil Engineer
7	Asst. Civil Engineers
1	Mechanical Inspector
1	Electrical "
1	Elevator "
1	Orn. Iron "
1	Caulking "
1	Inspector (General)
2	Expediters
1	Timekeeper
1	Asst. "
2	Cost Clerks
2	Clerks
1	Production Clerk
2	Distribution Clerks
27	Checkers
2	Storekeepers
31	Watchmen
1	Porter
1	Engineer (Quantities)
88	

16	Supervising Overhead
88	Operating
104	

1	Carpenter Foreman
2	Deputies
10	" Pushers
269	Carpenters
10	Carpenter Apprentices
1	Lather Foreman
1	Deputy
32	Lathers
326	

Carpenters: Continued on form work as follows: Making and placing floor arch forms on 54th and 55th flrs. - Making forms for beam sides, 1st bsmnt. - for beams and slab, Otis Elevator machine room, 21st flr. for column fireproofing - for underpinning under 5th Ave. sidewalk - for house pump and ejector foundations - for around electrical risers, and also making and placing forms at discontinued hoist shaft openings.

No.Men: (contd)	Remarks (contd)
326 Brot.Fwd. -	

2 Bricklayer Foremen	-(Carpenters - Contd)
8 " Deputies	Pushing laborers stripping forms on 50th fl. -
281 Bricklayers	patching forms. Placing grounds on 10,11,13,14
10 " Apprentices	16,17,18 flrs. Continued placing temporary pro-
9 Bricklayer Lab.Push.	tection at fire stairs,hoists,radiators. A.B.
391 " Laborers	See Temporary elevators,at other openings and
1 General Labor For.	at limestone set. Placing hoist rails.Building
1 Arch Labor Foreman	fireproof doors for splice boxes.Raising and
11 Arch Labor Pushers	setting concrete hoppers at hoists. Continued
334 Arch Laborers	on temporary elevator cabs and on resturant,
1 Stone Setter Foreman	47th flr. Changing shoring on 33d St. & 5th Ave.
2 " " Deputies	sides. Dismantling hoist #6,also bucket hoist,
39 " Setters	Bldg.framework to support stone over openings
4 " Cutter Deputies	on 4th flr.- mine hoist shanty on 40th flr. -
32 " Cutters	boxes for fire plugs to street. Sheet piling in
	pier holes.Misc.repairing and cutting
1 Derrickman Foreman	Lathers: Clipping beams,55th flr.-Rolling out
5 " Pushers	reinforcing wire mesh and placing chairs over
123 Derrickmen	flr.arch forms 54th flr. Placing spandrel stir-
43 Carpenter Helpers	rups and ceiling hangers on 53d flr. and 54th fl.
1 Excavator Pusher	Placing reinforcing steel at discontinued hoist
44 Excavators	openings,and for slab under elev.mchry.21st fl.
1 Driller Pusher	Wrapping wind bracers 32nd fl. & sub.bsmnt. -
15 Drillers	beams in elev.shafts,15th & 17th flrs. and
	columns, 1st flr.
1 Cement Fin.Pusher	Bricklayers: Backing up exterior limestone and
49 Cement Finishers	metal 4th,38th & 39th stories. Building fire
1 Pipefitter Foreman	tower,30th flr. Cleaning face brick of same.
3 Pipefitters	Setting terra cotta partitions around elev.shfts.
1 Elev.Const.Pusher	stairs,toilet rooms, etc.first bsmnt.27th,28th
5 " Constructors	and 29th flrs. Laying out terra cotta partition
12 " " Helpers	in 1st bsmnt. Furring columns.Pointing up and
	cleaning down elev.shafts.
1 Ironwork Pusher	Bricklayer Laborers: Mixing mortar -tending
9 Ironworkers	bricklayers-handling materials-scaffold work for
1 Master Mechanic	both bricklayers & stone setters. Helping carp-
25 Hoisting Engineers	enters on column forms & on protection.Sweeping
2 Asst. " "	flr.arches. Picking up scrap wood & cleaning up
3 Plasterer Laborers	after bricklayers. Pouring stone concrete at
3 Rockmen	old retaining wall,2nd bsmnt. Cutting rock for
1 Burner	retaining wall,also for piers under 34th St. in
2 Maintenance Men	sidewalk vault area.Laying temp.tracks for indus-
20 Water Boys	trial railroad in bldg.for Koppel cars carrying
1824	materials.
	Arch Laborers: Pouring cinder concrete arches on
1928 Carried Fwd.	52nd and 53d flrs., completing the 52nd.Pouring

stone concrete underpinning 5th Ave. side at old
brick retaining wall,also pouring stone concrete
flr. slab in motor room, 21st flr. Stripping
flr.arch forms on 49th & 50th flrs. Stripping
misc.forms. Helping carpenters, lathers & cement finishers. Moving hoppers. Handling protection nets, tarpaulins and lumber for elev.shaft
protection.Sweeping & watering forms.Fire patrol.
Loading dirt trucks from chute main flr. Signalmen on hoists.
Stone Setters: Setting ext.limestone walls,4th &
39th stories.Setting Cowie pressure plates.Point-
ing up & washing down limestone.

Remarks

No.Men :

Starrett Brothers and Eken - Contd.

1928   Brot.forward

Stone Cutters: Trimming and fitting limestone. Cutting
Lewis and anchor holes, 40th and 5th flrs.Recutting
raglet to allow for caulking.

Derrickman: Manning guy derrick and stiff leg derricks,
6th flr. setback, handling and distributing limestone.
Raising swinging scaffolds. Raising crabs.

Carpenter Helpers: General sweeping up inside and outside of building. Tending temporary job telephones on
20th, 30th and 40th flrs. Painting numbers on columns
and floor numbers on stairs. Stencilling "E.S." on
windows. Tending water barrels. Helping in storeroom.
Distributing anchors to stone setters.

Excavators - Rockmen: Cleaning out trench under sub-
basement for waterproofing. Excavating for refrigera-
tor room flr. - also for pier holes for sidewalk vault
columns under 5th Ave. Carrying lumber. Cleaning out
scrap iron. Carrying guns and hose for drillers.

Drillers: Drilling in pier holes for sidewalk vault
columns and retaining wall under 5th Ave. Cutting
out ejector compressor foundations - also for refriger-
ator foundations. Line drilling under 5th Ave. Repairing guns and hose.

Cement Finishers: Patching arches after stripping
forms - levelling arches at electrical duct locations-
fireproofing wind braces, sub-bsmnt. and 31st flr.
Patching beams in elevator shafts, 16th and 17th flrs.
Levelling concrete slab under elev.machinery 21st flr.

Pipefitters: Maintaining water lines - air lines -
Tending steam syphons and pump. Hooking up water to
hoist engines on 24th flr.

Maintenance Men: Continued on general maintenance of
of misc.job equipment.

Elevator Constructors: Continued on the installation
and extending height of temporary passenger mine hoists
Wiring west shaft - changing beams - placing brackets
and guide rails - Moving west hoist to 50th flr., machinery on same on 40th floor.

Ironworkers: Manning guy derrick hoisting stone, Lumber and material for Comstock (electricians). Placing
mine hoists motor on 40th flr. Moving out and loading
concrete mixer on truck. Moving out hoist engine from
2nd flr. Changing cables in hod hoists. Repairing
concrete bucket, and shifting and lashing down hoist
engine, 42nd flr.

Hoisting Engineers: Continued on operation of engines
for hoists and derricks. Two men on night fire watch.

Asst.Hoistg.Engnrs: Continued on operation of overhead cranes for handling limestone.

Plasterer Laborers: Cleaning up after plasterers.

Burner: Continued burning angle irons for hoists.
Misc.burning for pier holes.Repairing bucket hoist.

1928 Total - Starrett Brothers and Eken, Inc.

No.Men:	Remarks

SUB-CONTRACTORS
(Temporary Light and Power)

J.LIVINGSTON & CO.:
 1 Foreman   -continued on maintenance of temporary light
28 Electricians   and power
—
29

POST & McCORD, Inc.:   (Structural Steel Erection)
  1 Foreman   - All derrick gangs receiving and erecting
  1 Asst Foreman   59th & 60th flr.steel. Plumbing 57th & 58th
  9 Ironwork Pushers   floor columns. Bolting 57th flr.beam connec-
236 Ironworkers   tions. 18 gangs riveting 56th & 57th flr.beam
  9 Hoisting Engineers   connection to cols., beam connections within
  1 Compressor Engineer   3" of column centres, beam connections sup-
  1 Civil Engineer   porting other beams, and column splices at
  1 Timekeeper   56th flr. Painting 56th & 57th flr.steel.El-
  1 Checker   ectricians connecting up hoists on 52nd flr.
  6 Painters   and running feeders.
  6 Electricians
—
272

FREDERIC dep.HONE & CO.:   (Structural Steel Inspection)
  1 Inspector   - Inspection of steel as received & erected.

OTIS ELEVATOR CO.:   (Elevators)
Construction: - Setting brackets at 55th flr. - Rails and
  4 Foremen   conduits 52nd flr. - Lining up rails, 35th to
 98 Mechanics   45th flrs. Setting machines at 45th flr.,
113 Helpers   Bank D, and secondary sheaves and governor
                             supports at 44th flr. Piping and wiring in
                             Banks B & C. Installing car slings, Bank E.
                             Working in pits, on steel tape, and governor
                             sheaves. Cables Bank A.

Signals:
  1 Genl. Foreman   - Bank A: Hooking up selectors. Bank B: Pull-
  1 Foreman   ing and hooking up wires. Bank D: Setting
 26 Electricians   boxes and pulling wires. Bank E: Running
—   lantern risers. Bank F: Hooking up centre.
243   Bank G: Piping centre and running risers.

L.K.COMSTOCK & CO.:   (Electrical Work)
  1 Supt.   - Working on the following: Panels, feeders
  1 Foreman   and feeder conduits in basement - High ten-
  6 Asst Foremen   sion cables at 41st flr. Fire Alarm & Watch-
 67 Wiremen   man's clock, 30th flr. - Shaft lighting,29th
 32 Helpers   flr.up - Under-floor ducts,16th flr. -Nip-
  2 Apprentices   pling on partitions, 29th flr. Outlets on
  1 Timekeeper   17th flr. Conduits on 54th flr.
—
110

J.L.MURPHY, INC.:   (Plumbing)
  1 Foreman   - Continued on fire lines, 55th flr. -Soil
  1 Asst.Foreman   stacks to 43d flr. - Risers to 44th flr.
102 Plumbers   Branches 40th flr. - Vents, 39th flr. Toilet
 92 Helpers   room water supply branches, 38th flr. - Suc-
—   tion Tank in basement - Fire Pump, 20th flr.
196   29th floor loop.

851 Carried Fwd. -

No.Men: Remarks

   Sub-Contractors - Contd.
851 Brot Fwd. -

      BAKER, SMITH & CO.:   (Heating and Ventilating)
      Heating: - Installing sleeves, 55th flr. - Steam ris-
  1 Superintendent   ers, 40th flr. - 30th flr. riser transfers
  1 Foreman   drip lines on 5th flr. - Radiators and
 33 Mechanics   radiator branches, 6th flr. radiators,
 40 Helpers   21st flr. - 29th flr. main - 14" riser
                                     at 35th flr.

      Ventilating:
  1 Superintendent   - Continued on vertical flues, working on #1,
  3 Foremen   3,4, 87, 168, 182 and 202.
 43 Mechanics
 58 Helpers
  3 Draftsmen
  1 Apprentice

  1 Foreman
  4 Ironworkers   - Pencoyd Engineering Co. continued erecting
189   steel framing, platform and stairs between
                                     2nd & 4th flrs. southwest corner, for air
                                     filter system.

      Asbestos Const. Co.   -(Pipe covering Baker-Smith and Murphy Sub.)
  1 Foreman   Covering steam risers, 32nd flr. - water
 12 Mechanics   risers, 31st flr. - water branches 33d flr.
 10 Helpers   main shaft, steam and water risers 30th fl.
 23   32nd flr. steam branches, 21st flr. Ducts
                                     on 3d, 4th and 5th flrs.

      C.E.HALBACK & CO.:   (Arch.Iron Ext.Metal Trim & Spandrels 34th
  1 Foreman   St. and West Elevations)
  3 Mechanics   - Erecting stringers and platforms 54th to
  3 Helpers   55th flr. Stair #4
  1 Apprentice

  2 Foremen
 13 Mechanics   - Setting trim to 51st flr. Spandrels at
  9 Helpers   45th flr.
  1 Apprentice

  1 Foreman   - Handling materials for interior and
  5 Mechanics   exterior work
 39

      WM.H.JACKSON CO.:   (Exterior Metal Trim & Spandrels 33d St.
  1 Foreman   and 5th Ave. Elevations)
 17 Mechanics   - Setting trim to 51st flr. - Spandrels at
 16 Helpers   48th flr.
  1 Apprentice
 35

      JACOB RINGLE & SON: (Roofing and Sheet Metal Work)
  1 Foreman   - Repairing flashing at 30th flr. setback.
  1 Helper
  2

1139 Carried   Fwd

Daily Job Activity (continued)

No.Men: Remarks

Sub-Contractors - Contd.
1139 Brot fwd.

CAMPBELL METAL WINDOW CORP.: (Metal Window Frames and Sash)
1 Foreman   - Setting metal window frames,
1 Asst Foreman   fourth story
18 Mechanics
20

DAHLSTROM METALLIC DOOR CO.: (Elevator Enclosures)
1 Foreman   - Installing brackets,54th fl.-Saddles,
1 Asst Foreman   angles, and headers Bank D, to 29th
18 Mechanics   fl. - Bank A facias. Bucks 36th and
5 Helpers   37th fl.
3 Carpenters
28

LONG ISLAND WIRE WORKS: (Wire Mesh and Gates)
2 Mechanics   - Continued installing wire mesh screens
                                   and gates at hoists.

METAL DOOR & TRIM CO.:   (Metal Doors and Trim)
1 Foreman   - Setting bucks in basement and at
6 Mechanics   31st floor.
2 Laborers
9

CEMENT FINISH COMPANY: (Hydrolithic Waterproofing)
1 Foreman   - Continued applying waterproofing
6 Masons   finish coat to walls and floor, 33d St.
15 Laborers   side, sub-basement. Chipping walls and
22   columns for waterproofing.

HYDRO-BAR CORPORATION: (Dampproofing)
1 Foreman   - Applying dampproofing coat on walls,
9 Mechanics   31st floor.
10

EV-AIR TIGHT CALKING CO.:   (Window Caulking)
1 Foreman   - Continued caulking between steel trim
5 Mechanics   and stone and outside of window frames,
6   working between 8th & 17th flrs., and
                                   at 30th,31st and 34th floors.

WASHINGTON CONCRETE CORP.:   (Floor Fill and Finish)
1 Foreman   - Continued on 15th floor.
35 Masons
1 Laborer Foreman
35 Laborers
72

1308 Carried Fwd -

Daily Job Activity (Continued)

No.Men: Remarks
    Sub-contractors - Contd.

1308 Brot Fwd -

    MARTIN CONROY & SONS: (Lathing and Plastering)
    Lathing: - Continued on lathing and corner beads,
    1 Foreman   10th to 17th floor
   45 Lathers
    3 Laborers

    Plastering: - Browning in toilets, 9th and 10th flrs.
    1 Superintendent   and ceilings and walls, 12th and 13th flrs.
    1 Foreman   White Finish coat on 7th and to 11th flrs.
   78 Plasterers   Cement finish coat on 9th and 10th flrs.
   48 Laborers   st service spaces
  ───
  177

    TRAITEL MARBLE COMPANY: (Interior Marble)
    1 Foreman   - Continued setting base, Bank A elevator
    1 Setter   lobby, 7th floor.
    1 Foreman Helper
    3 Helpers
  ───
    6

    CONTRACTORS GLASS COMPANY: (Glass and Glazing)
    1 Foreman   - Glazing windows on 30th floor
   11 Glaziers
  ───
   12

    TUTTLE ROOFING COMPANY: (Temporary Covering over Finished Floors)
    2 Foremen   - Placing temporary felt covering over
    4 Helpers   finished floors in basement and on 14th
  ───   and 15th floors
    6

    L.S.FISCHL'S SONS: (Temporary Painting)
                                   Continued repainting street bridge,
    2 Painters   working on 5th Ave. side

1511 Total - Subcontractors

            Starrett Brothers and Eken, Inc. ----------1928 Men
            Subcontractors ------------------------------1511 "

                    Total --------------------3439 Men

                        J.W.Bowser,
                        Superintendent

Concrete Hoist Bucket loaded from Concrete Mixer - 2nd Basement.

Concrete for the floor slabs was mixed in the building basement in a batching plant set up for the construction. The concrete hoist was dedicated to one use: carrying buckets full of fresh concrete from the batching plant to the floor where concrete was being placed. (#331 10/22/30)

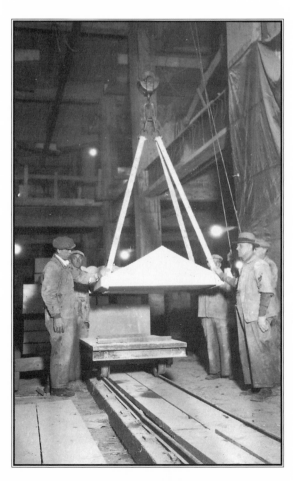

Mono-Rail Hoist carrying stone to flatcar. - 1st floor.

The monorail hoist was a material hoist with an overhead winch set on a small trolley, capable of moving back and forth. This hoist was used for carrying large, heavy items that could not be loaded and unloaded by hand, such as sections of stone. (#348 10/30/30)

Plant and Equipment:

A very important factor and one that contributes largely to the ultimate success of a building project of this magnitude, is the selection of the right kind of plant and equipment, together with its proper location.

A well planned equipment layout, designed to serve the needs of all parts of the construction work in the most efficient and economical manner, is one of the first important problems confronting the Job Superintendent.

The principal equipment items considered by the Builders, after the foundations had been completed were the following:

Temporary passenger elevators and Mine Cage passenger hoists
Material hoists
Concrete and Mortar mixing machinery for Floor Arches, Basement Walls and Sub-basement floor and Masonry. Overhead Mono-rail Trolley System for unloading materials on main floor.
Industrial Railway System for distributing materials.
Stone erection equipment.
Steel Guy Derricks for lifting heavy machinery.
Saw Rigs and Saw Filing Machine.

A description of the various types of equipment outlined above will be treated in the following paragraphs.

Inside Material Hoists Used:

The choice of an inside hoisting system was made largely on account of the ample floor areas within the building. The lower floors from sub-basement to 5th floor are each approximately, 425 ft. by 197 ft. This size is reduced slightly by setbacks until the main tower shaft is reached at the 30th fl. level and from that point up to the 86th floor, main roof, the area of each floor is approximately 185 ft. by 134 ft.

This condition made bays accessible within the building that could be used for temporary shaft openings without undue interference with mechanical construction work.

A study of comparative costs was made between the inside method and the outside method of all steel hoist shaft construction on the exterior of the building.

It was proved satisfactorily that by using the inside method of bracketing the guide rails of the hoist shafts to the steel structure and building wire screen protection enclosures around each floor opening, a substantial saving in money would be effected. This method, of course, had to include in its cost the excess expense involved in returning to patch the concrete floor arches, finish cement floors and plastering, in order to fill in the temporary floor openings after the hoisting system had been discontinued.

All of the limestone from the 6th floor setback to the 86th floor roof was cut in sizes that could be raised easily in material hoists, so it was decided to hoist practically everything on these material hoists, except, of course, the structural steel and the few large machinery units that had to be raised by the steel derricks.

Considering the height of the building and the heavy duty to be imposed on these hoisting units, a type of engine had to be selected that had qualities of speed and durability and a car that had extra sturdiness of construction to withstand the heavy loads to be placed upon it.

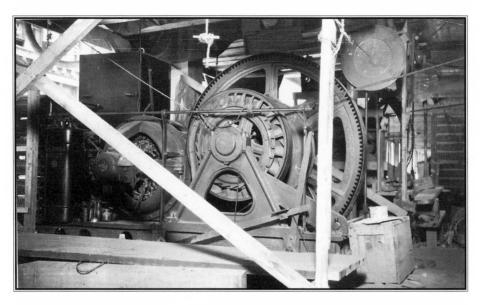

Thomas Hoist Engine. 200 H.P., A. C., single drum, single cable,
8800-lb. lift at 600 F.P.M. Operates Material Hoists.

*Materials hoists used in construction may look very much like primitive elevators but
do not require the safety features or relatively low acceleration of passenger elevators.
Instead of the complex cabling and safety devices of an elevator, the hoist engine is simply a large electric motor with a single cable wrapped around a drum. (#199 7/12/30)*

Unloading Sheet Metal from hoist - on
84th floor.

*Relatively small, light elements that could be
loaded by hand were placed on a materials
hoist and sent to the floor where they were
needed. (#355 10/29/30)*

PLANT AND EQUIPMENT (Continued)

Types of Hoisting Machinery Used:

Six hoisting engines were selected - made by Thomas Elevator Co. of Chicago - to form the first series of material hoisting units.

Each of these engines was of 200 H.P., capable of hoisting a load of 8000 lbs. at a rate of 600 feet per minute. This engine is known as Type F-911-A, high speed single reduction, single drum of the band friction type - complete with Thomas Automatic Motor Brakes. Each hoist is equipped with G.E. 200 H.P., 3 phase, 60 cycle, 220 volt continuous rated slip ring motors with variable speed controllers and dial indicators. Drum shell to give 1200 per minute with 400 lbs.

In conjunction with the above six hoisting engines, two concrete buckets and four steel platform cages were used.

The two buckets were Lakewood Type L-31 cubic feet capacity, 28 c.f. working capacity.

The four cages were built by the Union Iron Works of Hoboken, N.J. Each cage had platform 5',4½" face to face of guides, or 5'11 5/8" wide overall by 6'6" deep. The clear height from platform to inside of upper cross member 8 ft. Hinged roof shields covered with heavy wire mesh - Platform provided with 24" gauge track with car wheel locking dogs to operate from either side - Each cage provided with landing dogs built into platform and arranged to be operated from either end of platform. When sliding bars or levers are not engaged to hold the dogs out, dogs will be held within platform by means of springs. Side of cages covered with heavy wire mesh for their entire height. No coverings or bars at the front or rear. Cars built for maximum load of 6800 lbs. Weight per cage 2100 lbs.

The shaftheads in each of these hoist shafts were constructed of 12" by 12" timbers. The main sheave in each shafthead was a 48" diameter steel sheave with oil reservoir for 3/4" wire rope; 3½" by 22" steel shaft and two heavy type babbitted pillow blocks, equipped with sight feed lubricators

The shaft heads were raised as required to keep pace with the ever mounting structural steel - generally, five floors each time.

These units were supplemented on the job requirements demanded until the maximum service reached 17 hoisting units, as follows:-

Shaft Range	Hoisting Engine Used	Type of Car	Engine Placed
2nd Bsmnt to 20th floor	60 H.P.Lidgerwood	Platform	
2nd Bsmnt to 21st floor	60 H.P.Lidgerwood	Platform	
2nd Bsmnt to 21st floor	60 H.P.Lidgerwood	Platform	
2nd Bsmnt to 65th floor	100 H.P.Lidgerwood	Bucket	
2nd Bsmnt to 72nd floor	65 H.P.Lidgerwood	Platform	
2nd Bsmnt to 80th floor	100 H.P.Lidgerwood	Platform	
2nd Bsmnt to 80th floor	100 H.P.Lidgerwood	Platform	
2nd Bsmnt to 80th floor	200 H.P.Thomas	Bucket	
2nd Bsmnt to 80th floor	200 H.P.Thomas	Bucket	
2nd Bsmnt to 80th floor	200 H.P.Thomas	Platform	
2nd Bsmnt to 80th floor	200 H.P.Thomas	Platform	
2nd Bsmnt to 80th floor	200 H.P.Thomas	Platform	
2nd Bsmnt to 80th floor	200 H.P.Thomas	Platform	

Rocker Dumpcar being loaded with brick from hopper. - 1st Basement.

The dumpcar was loaded with brick from the hopper with little work required by the two laborers present. (#177 6/18/30)

Rocker Dumpcar load of brick being rolled onto Material Hoist. - 1st Basement.

The dumpcar was then rolled onto the materials hoist, where it would be lifted to the floor where the load was required and rolled on the track on that floor. (#160 6/18/30)

PLANT AND EQUIPMENT (Continued)

Types of Hoisting Machinery Used - Continued

Relay Hoists - 77th to 86th Floors

Shaft Range	Hoisting Engine Used	Type of Car	Engine Placed
77th to 86th floor	100 H.P.Lidgerwood	Bucket	
77th to 86th floor	100 H.P.Lidgerwood	Platform	
* 77th to 86th floor	60 H.P.Lidgerwood	Platform	
* 77th to 86th floor	60 H.P.Lidgerwood	Platform	

* These two also served Mooring Mast construction above 86th floor level.

Wire Screen Protection Around all Hod Hoist Openings:

Heavy wire mesh panels, manufactured by the Long Island Wire Works, were placed on two sides of each material hoist opening on each floor and around the passenger elevator and Mine cage shaft openings. The four sides of passenger hoist shafts were completely covered with these panels with suitable sliding gates for entrance to cars. These panels were attached to wooden studding.

Electric Material Hoist Control System:

The method in general use whereby gong signals are given to engineer on hoisting engine by means of signalman pulling a bell cord, was entirely superseded by a system devised by one of the electricians working on the building. This is known as the Bedell System and was used on this building for the first time.

The up-signalman or down-signalman by pressing a button, automatically rings a gong attached to the hoisting engine in a panel box in front of the engineer. A green light flashes simultaneously thereby giving a sound and sight signal at the same time. A portable telephone used in conjunction with the signal lines also keeps both signalmen and engineer in communication if conversation is required.

A brief description of the equipment used in this system and its mode of operation follows:

Equipment for Engineer: Consists of a small steel cabinet in which is a panel. This cabinet is placed directly opposite engineer in direct line of his vision. The panel contains a gong, switches, relays and lamps, operated by the same feed that operates the engine. A.C.current is preferable for operation but D.C.current can be used. A.C.current was used on this bldg.

Equipment for Signalmen: Each signalman has a small steel box which contains a button and buzzer and this box is held at side of the man by means of a shoulder strp. A small combination telephone set enables him to get in verbal communication with engineer or other signalman, as required.

Operation: The left side of cabinet which has a green lamp and a red lamp, is controlled by the down signalman. When he presses his button the gong rings and green light flashes to give the engineer sound and sight signal. At the same time the signalman hears his buzzer record the fact that the signals have been received by the engineer. The red lamp lights only when the signalman removes his plug from socket and shows that system is not in operation.

Rocker Dumpcar (Koppel) on track to brick hopper.

Materials not easily damaged, especially common brick, could be handled quickly and roughly using a Rocker Dump Car—literally, a hoist car that could be tipped to one side to dump out its contents. The car was rolled on the track below the brick hopper in the first basement, which contained brick loaded from the first-floor level above. (#112 5/17/30)

PLANT AND EQUIPMENT (Continued)

Electric Material Hoist Control System - Continued

Safety Feature: The system is safe because only the signalman can transmit the required signals to the engineer from a control unit directly in his possession.

Speed: The system is fast because it is easier to transmit on electric signal in any weather condition. The rope systems now in general use are affected by the weather.

Accuracy: All signals are supervised and attract the engineer by both sight and sound. The gong operated, returns the signal to the bellman in the sound of a buzz. An additional check can be made at any time by telephone, if necessary.

Flexibility: Control lines can be lengthened to suit any condition.

The Signals for Two and Three Drum Hoists:

The Bedell two or three drum engine signal, while incorporating all desirable features of the material hoist control, is necessarily different in operation.

It has a gong for each drum on the engine and as each gong is of a different size, it vibrates at a different frequency and in turn actuates the synchronized buzzer of the signalman's unit accordingly. It thereby gives distinct buzzer sounds for each different size bell operated.

A safety feature , consisting of a trouble buzzer, operates through a relay in the event of a cable breakage.

The system is very fast in operation and requires but one operator, thereby eliminating relay signals.

The Tirex rubber cables used on these systems function satisfactorily under all weather conditions and either system, being designed for portable use, can be set up very rapidly.

The inventor is Frank H.Bedell, 2107 Bedford Avenue, Brooklyn, N.Y.

Industrial Track on 72nd floor.

Tracks were laid on each floor as soon as the concrete slab was complete. This section of track on the 72nd floor clearly is near the outer edge of the slab on the right, with a flat car at the other end of the building. (#263 9/17/30)

Industrial Track (12-lb. 26-gauge rail) on 85th floor.

Industrial railway tracks on the uppermost office floor. (#326 10/17/30)

PLANT AND EQUIPMENT (Continued)

Concrete Mixing Plant:

For the concrete floor arch construction, two units were used as follows

Two 21-S (3/4 yard capacity) Ransome Standard Building Mixers on skids, each equipped with 15 H.P. - A.C. General Electric Motor "Housed", also containing batchhopper and water measuring tank complete.

Two (2) #240 (40 cubic feet) Ransome Steel Floor Hoppers
Three (3) #203 (60 " ") " " " " "

Blaw-Knox Batchers and Hoppers used in connection with Mixers:

1 #104   Bin-12½ cubic yard, heaped capacity, 19 tons
1 401   Batcher - 21 to 28½ cubic feet capacity
1 300   Batcher - 9 to 21 cubic feet capacity
1 201   Volume Batcher for Wood Bin - Capacity 6 to 9-5/10 cu.ft.

All the necessary concrete chutes and accessories were Ransome equipment.

The above units were increased by 4 3/4-yd. Marsh Capron Concrete Mixers used for pouring basement walls, floor on ground and supplementing the concrete floor arch units on the large floor areas. A small portable 3½ cu.ft. capacity tilting gasoline driven mixer was used for pouring concrete column fireproofing in 2nd and 1st basements and first floor.

For mixing mortar for Stone, Brick and Terra cotta and miscellaneous concrete patching work, the following mixers were used:

1 No.4865 Jaeger, 1-Bag capacity concrete mixer, trailer type
1 49431   "   1 "   "   "   "   "   "

Overhead Trolley System:

For the purpose of unloading stone from trucks within the bldg. four sections of overhead mono-rail 15" I Beam, 42.9 lbs. per ft. were installed at convenient points and operating along same were four 4-Ton Chisholm-Moore Electric Hoists, equipped with 5 H.P., A.C. 220 volts, 3-phase, 60 cycle Motors - working load 8000 lbs. - lift 12 ft. single speed - equipped with Timken bearings. Manufactured by Chisolm-Moore Elec.Hoist Co.

Practically all of the exterior limestone was unloaded by this system and trucked on flat cars to the inside hoists for raising and distribution on the various floors.

Industrial Railway Equipment:
In connection with the Industrial Railway System used for distributing materials, the following equipment was selected, all manufactured by the Koppel Industrial Equipment Corporation:
24, all steel, double side Rocker Dump Cars "Koppel", 2100 cu.ft. capacity 12 Gauge - approximate weight of each car 1150 lbs.
24 Platform Cars "Koppel", 2 to 3 ton capacity for 24" Gauge Track
31 "Koppel" Standard Cast Iron Ball-bearing Turntables, 44" Dia.of 3½ ton capacity
4000 ft. "Koppel" Standard Straight Portable Track, suitable for 24" gauge in standard sections 15 ft. long with five steel ties per section.
360 ft. Curved Track - 12 ft. radius "Koppel".
6 Portable Switches, 3 right hand and 3 left hand switches 9 ft. long.

Track, Turntable and Flatcar - load of Limestone on 85th floor.

The track for the materials hoist cars was, in effect, a miniature railroad. The track had the same profile as actual railroads, but was roughly one-tenth the weight; the distance between the rails was slightly less than one-half standard track gauge; and intersections had wyes and turntables similar to those used for any set of rails. (#327 10/17/30)

PLANT AND EQUIPMENT (Continued)

Stone Erection Equipment:

30 Dobbie Hand Power Winches #6324, capacity 1200 lbs. with 4"x16" Drums were used for setting stone in all stories above setback at 6th floor. All of this stone was raised by inside material hoists, except a number of large stones at top of building which had to be lifted by steel erection derrick on 86th floor roof.

10 No.228, 3-ton capacity, Stiff Leg Saugen Derricks, each with 36 ft. boom, were placed on 6th floor setback to lower stone for setting 2nd to 5th stories. Horton Lewises and Crabs were used to furnish lifting grip in all stones.

Steel Guy Derricks:

In order not to interfere with the erection derricks of Post & McCord, the steel erectors, a 15-ton Terry Steel Guy Derrick, operated by 90 H.P. Double Drum Lidgerwood Hoist, was placed on 6th floor setback roof on 34th St. side at northwest end of building.

At 25th floor setback roof on 5th Ave. and 33d St. southeast corner, a 10-ton Terry Steel Guy Derrick, operated by a 65 H.P. Double Drum Lidgerwood Hoist was also set.

Considerable form lumber for concrete floor arches and machinery too large for inside material hoists were raised by these derricks in the early stages of the operation when interference with the regular steel erection derrick could be least afforded.

Saw Rigs and Filing Machinery:

For cutting lumber for floor arch forms and for general use, the following were selected:

1 No.3, B.P. "Wappett" Electric Saw
1   4, S.B. "Wappett"   "   "
1 C H & E No.14 Saw Rig complete, equipped with 15 H.P. Gasoline Engine
1 Model F-5 "Foley" Saw Filer, equipped with special 115 volt, DC motor
1 Band Saw Machine
1 Cross Cut Saw Machine

1ˢᵗ Basement
Equipment Layout

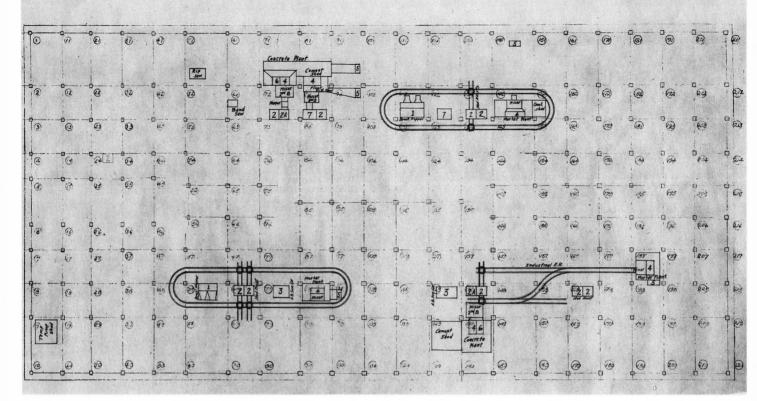

	LEGEND
=	Industrial R.R.
1	Brick Hopper
2	Hod Hoist
2A	Concrete Bucket
3	A.B. See Cars
4	Sand Hopper
5	Cement Slide
6	Cinder Slide
7	Hod Hoist Below
	Mine Hoist

Construction Equipment 1ˢᵗ Floor

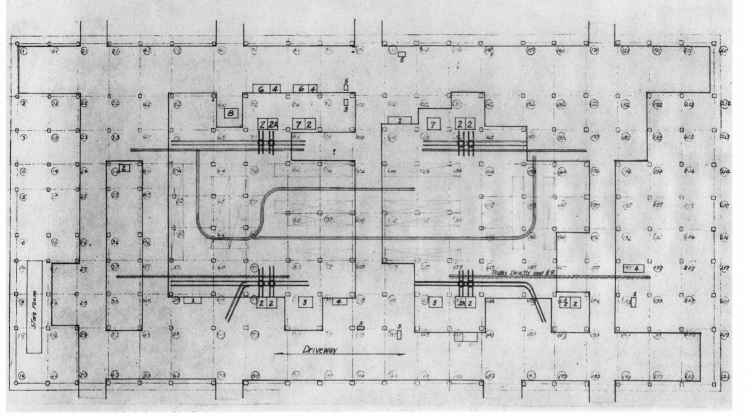

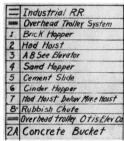

	Industrial R.R
	Overhead Trolley System
1	Brick Hopper
2	Hod Hoist
3	A.B See Elevator
4	Sand Hopper
5	Cement Slide
6	Cinder Hopper
7	Hod Hoist below Mine Hoist
8	Rubbish Chute
	Overhead trolley Otis Elev Co
2A	Concrete Bucket

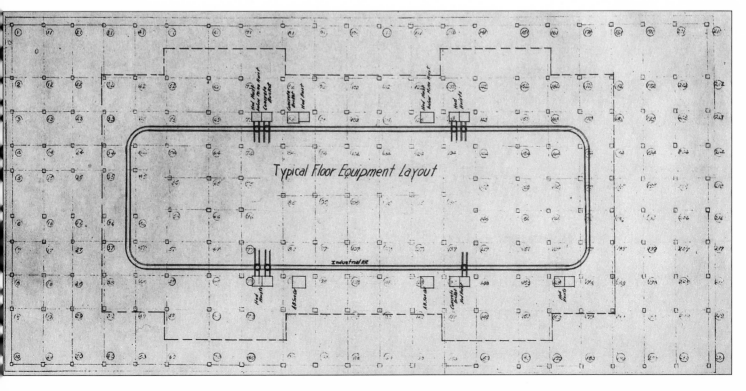

Typical Floor Equipment Layout

Dumping debris in Dirt Chute. - 9th floor.

Removing debris from the construction site was far easier than delivering new materials. Construction debris has no shape and cannot be damaged. The Dirt Chute was simply a shaft running vertically through the building, with doors that could be opened to empty a wheelbarrow. (#194 7/15/30)

Loading truck with debris from hopper
of Dirt Chute - 1st floor.

The bottom of the dirt chute was a hopper similar to that used for loading bulk materials into the dump cars. This hopper fed dump trucks that carried the debris from the site to disposal. (#195 7/15/30)

<u>PLANT AND EQUIPMENT</u> (Continued)

<u>Dirt Chute:</u>

In considering a dirt chute for the construction period, the decision was made that a wooden chute would not be used. Such a chute requires a larger opening in each floor arch which causes additional expense in the final patching of floor openings. It requires constant repairs on account of breakages, and, as a rule, allows considerable dust to escape.

<u>Steel Plate Chute Erected:</u>

A large bin was constructed of heavy timbers and made dust-proof on the second floor to receive all dirt and refuse. This bin fed through a floor opening into rubbish trucks on main floor.

The steel chute was extended from second floor to 85th floor as required and was 16" x 20" in size with a door opening at each floor for dumping in the dirt and rubbish. At each floor there were two supporting angle irons 3" x 2½" x 3/8".

From second to 11th floor the chute was made of 1/4" steel plate and from 11th floor to top, 3/16" steel plate was used.

The chute ran perpendicularly up through the building and served its purpose very well.

At the conclusion of the work, the chute can be salvaged and re-used, as it has suffered very little wear and tear.

Temporary Passenger Elevator No. 2
(A. B. See) - Running to 30th floor.

Four elevators, manufactured by A. B. See, were salvaged from the Waldorf-Astoria and used for slower local service during construction. (#219 7/25/30)

TEMPORARY ELEVATOR SERVICE

<u>Getting the Men up to their work:</u>

A very costly item on buildings of this character is caused by prematurely turning over for temporary operation permanent elevator cars before the work on the various units has been completely finished. This practice necessarily results in causing the elevator construction organization to work overtime on account of the cars being in temporary use during the day.

In order to avoid the payment of this excess time, and also to allow the elevator constructors unobstructed use of all the permanent shafts, it was decided to install an absolutely independent system of temporary elevators to take care of the passenger service during the construction period.

The steel framing plans provided for two independent shaft openings, properly braced and framed for the two Mine Cage Lifts, and also two independent shaft openings for the A.B.See cars. These openings extended from ground floor up to the 85th floor.

<u>Mine Cage Passenger Lifts:</u>

For quick installation, to meet the initial elevator requirements, two mine cage lifts were installed. As soon as the steel erection permitted, one of these units was installed and placed in operation from the first floor to the 10th floor. This car started operating on June 18, 1929. On this date, steel was erected to 21st floor, and floor arches were concreted to 18th floor.

On June 27th, the second mine cage lift was placed in operation from ground floor to 20th floor. On this date, steel was erected to 26th floor and concrete floor arches were poured to 25th floor.

These passenger cages were built for a load of 3500 lbs. and were enclosed on three sides with No.14 gauge steel sheets, and the front was enclosed one-half with the same material. The door on each car was arranged so that when not held closed with latches it would open and operate circuit breaker. Cages had roof shields, not hinged, and were provided with safety dogs which operate in case of the breaking of the main cable. Cage was also provided with a shock-absorber attached to lifting links.

In connection with these two mine cage passenger lifts, were used two special single drum electric hoists (Lidgerwood) each for a duty of 4200 lbs. on a single line pull at 300 feet per minute rope speed; equipped with motor of Electric Dynamic Company; two speed, No.262 Frame, continuous 60 H.P. 900 R.P.M., 20 H.P., 300 R.P.M., high torque type, arranged for A.C., 3 Phase, 60 Cycles, 220 Volts.

These two machines were set on 2nd floor and the hoists were equipped with all safety devices that are part of a standard electric elevator installation.

The engines were operated by experienced engineers, who remained at controls in machine rooms.

Elevator operators were on the cars. These operators gave signals to machine rooms and the signals were received in the form of colored lights. These colored lights indicated direction of travel required and floors upon which stops were to be made.

Cut-out switches in cars, also gate switches, prevented cars from being moved by engineers unless operators were ready, with gates closed and all danger hazzards eliminated. An erection gang was steadily employed to carry forward this installation as the steel erection work progressed.

These units were operated because it was considered they were the most

Temporary passenger Elevator No. 3 "Mine Hoist."

Six temporary elevators were installed during the course of the work. Two of them, the Mine Hoists, were the type of open car elevators used on most high-rise construction sites. This type of lift runs fast and roughly, but is capable of carrying large numbers of laborers. (#206 7/18/30)

flexible to use for quick installation to take care of the daily increasing
demands for raising the men to a reasonable height below the rapidly mounting steel structure, which ultimately reached an erection record of one
story per day.

On the date these two units were in operation, there were employed on the
building 2803 men.

The same type of shaft and method of construction were employed in connection with these two mine cage lifts as were used in the regular material
hoist construction. The guide rails were extended to a point above the overhead sheaves, so that operation of the cars below that point was carried on
while above the cathead sheaves the work of installing the rails to higher
levels proceeded. Whenever extension of travel was necessary on these
hoists the work was done at night without interruption of service for the
following morning. Extra parts and equipment were purchased to accomodate
this method of construction.

Temporary A.B.See Passenger Elevators and Otis Cars:

About five years before the Waldorf-Astoria Hotel was demolished, an
installation of four new A.B.See elevator units was made. These units were
in excellent condition, so the General Contractor decided to salvage them,
store unit needed, then reinstall for temporary use during the construction
period.

As soon as conditions would permit, a start was made on the installation
of two of these A.B.See elevator units to operate from ground floor to 30th
floor. In the same shaft openings, to operate from 34th to 64th floor,
work progressed on the second two A.B.See units.

The first two A.B.See cars running from ground floor to 30th floor, went
into operation on July 18th, 1930. The second two A.B.See cars, running
from 34th floor to 64th floor, went into operation on Sept.9, 1930.

The two Mine Cage cars were raised to different levels as conditions
required, and finally served from 64th to 78th floors.

The Otis Elevator Co. were able to turn over for temporary use two permanent cars running from sub-basement to 25th floor on July 21st, 1930 and
two more permanent cars running from ground floor to 43d floor on Aug.8,1930.

With the above ten cars in operation, ample facilities were provided for
all the needs for passenger service during the construction period.

Flexibility of Mine Cages Demonstrated:

The quick jumps of the Mine Cage units proved of great value in keeping
pace with the rapid advance of the steel erection, as shown in the following
study:

West Mine Cage Car	Steel Erected To:	East Mine Cage Car	Steel Erected To:
Travel-1st Fl.to 10th fl.	16th floor	1st flr. to 14th fl	20th floor
1st " " 20th fl.	26th floor	1st flr. to 24th fl.	30th floor
1st Fl. to 26th fl.	32nd floor	1st flr. to 30th fl.	36th floor

At this stage, Otis turned over the two cars to operate from sub-basement
to 25th floor, and the two A.B.See cars were in operation from first to
30th floor.

Temporary Elevator Service - Continued

Flexibility of Mine Cages Demonstrated - Continued.

West Mine Cage Car	Steel Erected To:	East Mine Cage Car	Steel Erected To:
		First to	
Travel-1st fl.to30th fl.	37th floor	(Remained) 30th fl.	37th floor

It was found that by keeping one car traveling several floors higher than the other car, the mechanics would all flock to the car of the highest level, thereby causing all the traffic to this particular car, and, consequently, delaying their getting to place of work.

To overcome this condition, it was decided that although the completion of one shaft would permit the car in that particular shaft to proceed to a higher level, we would not operate the car to the higher level, but keep the two cars always operating up to the same floor level. This meant even distribution of the men and less loss of time.

At this time it was found convenient to raise pits of both Mine Cages to permit travel to start at tenth floor.

West Mine Cage Car	Steel Erected To:	East Mine Cage Car	Steel Erected To:
Travel-10th fl.to 40th fl.	46th floor	10th fl. to 40th fl.	46th floor

When the pits of the Mine Cage units were raised to higher levels, the lower sections of both shafts became available for use of material hoist units. This program was carried out to the extent that eventually material hoists were operating in these shafts from basement to 63d floor at the time when Mine Cage units were ultimately operating from 64th to 78th floor.

Pits were next raised to 19th floor to permit travel to start at 20th floor:

West Mine Cage Car	Steel Erected To:	East Mine Cage Car	Steel Erected To:
Travel-20th fl.to 46th fl.	54th fl.	20th fl. to 46th fl.	54th floor

At this time the two hoisting engines operating the Mine Cage units were raised from 2nd floor to 40th floor. During this period there was a slight inconvenience, causing about twelve stories of walking, as it was necessary to dismantle and reassemble the two hoisting machines to get same to 40th floor level.

When this work was accomplished, the travel service was raised again as follows:

West Mine Cage Car	Steel Erected To:	East Mine Cage Car	Steel Erected To:
Travel-30th to 52nd fl.	61st floor	30th to 51st floor	63d floor
-30th to 66th fl.	66th floor	30th to 60th floor	68th floor

At this time, the second two A.B.See units were placed in operation from 34th to 64th floor.

West Mine Cage Car	Steel Erected To:	East Mine Cage Car	Steel Erected To:
Travel 43d to 64th fl.	70th floor	43d to 64th floor	70th floor
43d to 70th fl.	80th floor	43d to 70th floor	78th floor

At this time the two Otis elevators were put into operation from the first floor to the 43d floor.

Temporary Elevator Service - Continued

Flexibility of Mine Cages Demonstrated - Continued

Pits of Mine Cage units were raised to 63d floor, while lower section of shafts were still being used for material hoists.

West Mine Cage Car	Steel Erected to:	East Mine Cage Car	Steel Erected to:
Travel-64th to 74th fl.	82nd floor	64th to 74th floor	83d floor
64th to 78th fl.	86th floor	64th to 78th floor	86th floor

These two cars have been in operation for five months at time of this writing and are giving satisfactory service.

Due to union rules, the majority of men employed by the sub-contractors do not leave their lockers until 8 A.M.

To avoid too much congestion at this time, the General Contractors employed a stagger system, starting certain trades at 7 A.M. - others at 7:30 A.M.

Men stationed at the elevator entrance at the various relay points directed traffic and the service kept going very satisfactorily.

Terra Cotta tile ready for hoisting.

The rails provided an easy-rolling surface for the flat cart; laborers provided the "push." (#299 10/1/30)

1/2-bag Hand-tilting gasoline motor,
Concrete Mixer - for column fill.

When only small amounts of concrete were needed, a portable mixer was used on location. This one is pouring concrete into a buggy. (#145 6/11/30)

UNLOADING AND DISTRIBUTING MATERIALS

All the material (except structural steel) was received and unloaded on Main Floor of the building.

As soon as the main street floor concrete arch had set properly, a six inch decking of fir timber was laid for protection over areas to be used for driveways and material storage spaces around material hoists.

Driveways were about 25 feet in width and extended around the four sides of the Main Floor. Trucks could drive completely around the four sides with ample room for passing two abreast.

Contiguous to all the material hoists were ample spaces for unloading and temporary storage of materials before raising to upper floors.

Four entrances on 34th Street and three entrances on 33d St., afforded the required entrances and exits necessary to avoid congestion of trucks at any time within the building.

A check taken on a day when the work was nearing its most active stage, recorded a total of nearly 500 loads of various kinds of materials, machinery and equipment as having been unloaded within the building during the eight-hour period, and all this was accomplished without confusion or unnecessary delays. This total, of course, does not take into consideration the structural steel that was raised from trucks on 33d and 34th Streets by steel derricks on top of the structure.

Handling Common Bricks:

We are quite certain the method used in receiving and distributing common bricks on this building was a distinct innovation for a building operation of this type. Considering the height of the building and the enormous quantity (10,000,000 common bricks) required to be used almost entirely for backing up the exterior limestone and metal trim, the problem was to be equipped to raise the bricks fast enough to keep pace with the stone-setting and hold up to the schedule of at least one story enclosed per day. For a time, the rate accomplished was almost one and one-half stories per day.

It is no exaggeration to state that the bricks were untouched by human hands from the time they left the brickyard until the bricklayers picked them up to set down in place in the mortar.

Two brick hoppers were constructed in the First Basement. Each hopper had a capacity of about 20,000 bricks. Floor openings leading into these hoppers were made in Main Floor. Trucks driving into the building dumped the bricks into these floor openings which were conveniently located near entrances to the building.

Each hopper fed the bricks through a slot opening into Koppel Double Side Rocker Dump Cars; each car having a capacity of about 400 common bricks. The loaded cars were pushed along industrial railway in First Basement and swung on turntables on to material hoists. After being raised to proper floor, cars were pushed off hoist and sent along railway to point on floor where required for use by bricklayers in backing up the exterior limestone and metal trim.

Hopper for cement, sand and cinders.

A clear statement of the immense size of the building is the need for on-site concrete preparation and mixing. Over 62,000 cubic yards of concrete were used in creating the floor slabs. Since an ordinary concrete mixer truck carried only a few cubic yards, it would have been impractical to attempt the standard technique of delivering concrete from an outside batching plant. This picture shows the hopper feeding one of the two batching plants set up on site to mix the raw materials into usable concrete. (#110 5/17/30)

Ransome 3/4 cu. yd. Mixer (fed by hopper overhead) and 1 cu. yd. "Lakewood" Bucket for hoisting.

The overhead hopper feeds the concrete mixer and the bucket used to transport the mixed concrete for delivery upstairs. (#111 5/17/30)

Comparison Handling Common Brick, Old and New Methods:

As previously stated, 400 common bricks could be loaded into a dump car.
Under the old system, two hand-wheelbarrows would have been wheeled on to
material hoist, each barrow containing 50 common bricks. The total number of
bricks hoisted with each lift under the new method was 400, as compared with
100 bricks under the old system.

The production schedule required the raising of at least 100,000 bricks every
eight hours to keep a sufficient quantity of bricks placed in advance to
enable the bricklayers to carry out their part of the program of enclosing
at least one floor per day. The bricks were always in place on at least
three floors above floor where bricklayers were setting.

Two material hoists, working eight hours each per day, were able to raise the
100,000 bricks required and, in addition, raise sufficient mortar to keep the
bricklayers supplied.

Under the old system, one hoist could have raised 30,000 bricks in eight
hours and it is estimated four hoists, at least, would have been required
to raise the 100,000 bricks and the mortar.

Labor Saved by Use of New Method:

For loading purposes, under the old system, eight men are required at the
bottom and six men at the top, or a total of 14 men, including the bellmen.
Manning the four hoisting units which would have been required under this
old method, called for employment of 56 men for eight hours each.

Under the new system, five men were required at the bottom and four men at
the top, or a total of 18 men for eight hours each for the two hoists used.

A saving of 38 men per eight hour day was effected by using the system
described.

Handling Concrete Materials:

The two main concrete mixing plants were erected in the Second Basement. The
material was fed into these plants from two combination bins erected in First
Basement. These bins were each divided into two sections and were constructed to receive approximately 12 yds. of sand in one compartment and about 30
yards of cinders or crushed stone (according to the aggregate required) in
the other compartment.

Floor openings, properly grilled, were made in the Main Floor to receive the
materials dumped by trucks into these respective bins.

Cement was dumped in bags from trucks on Main Floor in spaces adjacent to the
openings for the two concrete material bins mentioned above, and then passed
through floor openings down chutes, after which bags were stacked convenient
to operators who were employed to open the bags and feed cement to the two
mixer plants.

Rolls of wire mesh, beam clips, hangers and haunch stiffners used for reinforcing concrete floor arches, were raised on the platform material hoist.
Floor arch lumber was raised, one load to a lift by the steel derricks to
the top from street and then lowered down through steel frames and placed on
floor required. Stripped forms were raised for rousing through temporary
floor openings by single drum 25 H.P. Whip hoisting engines.

Bricklayers laying Terra Cotta partitions around permanent Elevator Shaft. - 10th floor.

Interior partitions were built of terra cotta tile. This type of hollow clay block is non-combustible and stable, and holds plaster well without any additional lath. Masons laid up tile in the same way as brick. Here they make up the enclosure for an elevator shaft. (#196 7/15/30)

Flatcar loaded with Terra Cotta Tile ready for Material Hoist.

Terra cotta tile was transported on flat cars. While strong enough for use in partitions, the tiles were relatively fragile and would break if subjected to the kind of rough handling that brick received in the dump cars. (#298 10/1/30)

HANDLING TERRA COTTA, TILE AND FACE BRICK

Terra cotta tile of various sizes and face brick were unloaded from trucks on Main Floor by hand and stacked along railway spurs, where same could be loaded quickly on to Koppel platform cars which were pushed on to the material hoists and raised to the opper floors for further distribution with the aid of the industrial railway system.

A platform car holds 75 pieces of 6" partition tile and up to 175 pieces of 2" tile. The number of intermediate sizes varied accordingly.

The old two-wheelbarrow system accomodates 8 to 12 pieces of tile in each barrow.

The side rocker dump cars carried 21 cubic feet of mortar - the wheelbarrow method, 3½ cubic feet in each barrow.

The partition tile and face brick were kept stacked in advance on each of the three floors above where the bricklayers were setting the material.

Forecast of Quantities to be Placed on Floors in Advance:

A schedule was made showing the estimated quantities of the different sizes of tile, common brick and face brick required on each floor.

By following this schedule, it was possible to have stacked always, three floors ahead, the allotted quantities. This reduced the necessity of rehandling material to a minimum.

Quantities Involved:

An idea of the masonry quantities raised on these material hoists may be gained from the following figures:

Common Brick	10,000,000
Face Brick	800,000
6" Terra Cotta	900,000 pcs.
4" " "	210,000 "
3" " "	200,000 "
2" " "	500,000 "
8" " "	10,000 "

The concrete raised for the floor arches (not including fill and finish) amounted to 62,000 cubic yards.

Wire Mesh for floor arch reinforcement	2,900,000 sq.ft.
Beam Clips,	700,000 lin.ft.

Horton stone winch in operation.

During the construction of high rises, most of the materials can be brought up and set in place from within the building. Portions of the façade are the usual exception, especially in buildings with masonry exterior walls. Even though much of the stone was raised to the proper elevation using the system of interior hoists and flatcars, exterior winches such as the one in this photograph were needed for setting the stone into position. (#164 6/25/30)

Dobbie hand winch and block - on 13th floor.

A block of stone is being raised to its final position by an exterior winch. (#161 6/20/30)

Unloading and Raising Exterior Limestone:

Two material hoists were assigned in the beginning, and later one hoist was required to raise the limestone. All limestone from the sixth floor setback to the 85th story roof was of a size that could be loaded readily on flatcars and raised on these material hoists.

The stone unloaded from trucks inside the building was raised from trucks by our overhead mono-rail trolley system, placed on platform cars which were pushed onto material hoists and placed on the upper floors in proper locations with the aid of an industrial railway system.

Material was kept on three floors in advance of floor where stone-setters were working.

All limestone for the lower part of the building up to and including the 5th story, was raised by stiff leg derricks placed on the 6th floor setback.

Approximately 198,328 cubic feet of limestone was set on the exterior of the building.

48" Sheaves - showing typical framing for shaft heads on
Material Hoists. - 81st floor.

Any traction elevator—that is, any elevator hung from cables rather than being pushed up by hydraulic pistons—has a set of large sheaves at the top. This photograph shows the sheaves for two hoists and the wood and steel framing around them. This construction is similar in effect to a permanent elevator machine room, although cruder. (#295 9/27/30)

UNLOADING AND DISTRIBUTING MATERIALS - Continued

Unloading and Raising Materials for Sub-Contractors:

An almost infinite variety of materials were received and raised for some forty odd sub-contractors employed in erecting various component parts of the building.

The Otis Elevator Company erected a mono-rail system for unloading their machinery on the first floor and this mono-rail trolley with its traveling cranes could unload machinery and carry it to any elevator shaft required. The machinery was then hoisted up through the shaftways by means of temporary hoisting engines placed at the shaft heads on the different levels, and these temporary hoists were used until the permanent machines were installed and placed in temporary operation.

Some idea can be gained of the various kinds of materials raised for sub-contractors by glancing at the following list:-

Roofing and Sheet Metal Materials	Vitreous Glass Partitions for Toilets
Exterior Metal Spandrels and Trim	Painting and Decorating Materials
Metal Windows	and Supplies
Lathing and Plastering Materials	Elevator Supplies
Floor Fill and Finish	Plumbing Materials and Equipment
Finished Carpentry and Millwork	Heating and Ventilating Materials
Metal Doors and Trim	and Equipment
Elevator Enclosures	Electrical Materials and Equipment
Glass	Electrical Fixtures
Hardware	Refrigeration Equipment
Miscellaneous Iron	Vacuum Cleaning System Materials
Aluminum	Steel Shutters and Doors
Mail Chute Construction Materials	Toilet Accessories
Interior Marble	Cork Insulation and Soundproofing
Tile	Materials
Terrazzo Materials	Dampproofing Materials
	Caulking Materials
	Hydrozone System Equipment and
	Supplies

Assignment of Material Hoists to Sub-Contractors:

Certain sub-contractors, such as the plasterer and the floor fill and finish subcontractor, had material hoists definitely assigned to them. Each sub-contractor (who did not have certain hoists assigned for his exclusive use) was required to report to the Foreman in charge of the Main Floor the hoist required, designating same by its number and the day and number of hours it would be in use for raising his material. This information had to be given to our Floor Foreman not less than two days in advance.

The sub-contractor had to instruct the drivers when delivery could be made and at which hoist the goods had to be unloaded.

If a driver did not have this information he would not be allowed to drive into the building to unload his goods. This referred, of course, to bulk material items by the load and the shipper was always more than willing to have the driver supplied with the information which insured a quick-delivery and return of the truck. If by chance the information was lacking by the driver, the truck was not allowed to enter the building until he called up his own office or the office of the sub-contractor and secured the necessary information. This prevented the congestion of trucks in the building.

FIRE PROTECTION

Fire Alarm Boxes:

As the building progressed, a fire alarm box was installed on every floor from the 2nd Basement to the 5th floor inclusive and on every alternate floor from the 6th to the 85th floors inclusive.

By pulling a hook in a fire box an alarm registers in the Central Office of the National District Telegraph Company and is immediately relayed to Fire Department Headquarters. At least once, each night a special key is inserted in each fire alarm box which registers in the Central Office to indicate that the circuit is in working order and has not been broken during the day.

Night Watchman's Tour Stations:

Watchman Tour Stations were installed as required, by the National District Telegraph Company. Two stations were placed in each basement and four stations on each floor from the Main Floor to the 5th floor inclusive.

Two stations were placed on each floor from the 6th to the 85th inclusive. Each night watchman had to start his tour by punching a Transmitter Station which automatically registered in the Central Office the fact that he had started his tour. With a key he carried, he had to punch the next nine stations in proper sequence and then return to the Transmitter Box, where he signalled again to the Central Office that he had finished his tour. The intermediate stations were manual and had no connection with the Central Office but had to be punched in proper sequence with a special key with a revolving cylinder. If all the intermediate stations were not punched in proper sequence, the key would not operate the transmitter station. One watchman took care of every five floors.

All watchmen had to make half hourly tours from 5 P.M. to 7 P.M. and from 8 P.M. to 6 A.M. - hourly tours were made.

If the starting and stopping signals were not received when due in the National District Central Office, a telephone report of the fact was made by the Central Office to our Head Night Watchman, who immediately investigated the cause of the delinquency.

Independent 'phone calls were made every hour from the 5 watchmen covering zones where our interior telephone booths were located within the building, to the Head Night Watchman.

This watchman's tour system was in operation every night and also on Saturday, Sunday and Holidays, during the daytime.

When the steel structure was being erected an independent system of portable stations containing keys were used whereby our watchmen used Chicago Clocks from the highest floor where National District Telegraph System had been installed up to the floor where the steel derricks were resting. A special man was always assigned to floors where arch forms were being erected and also a man was assigned exclusively to floors where riveters had forges and floor planking protection for the steel workers had been laid.

Each watchman was equipped with a small portable fire extinguisher and large fire extinguishers were distributed on various floors, especially where there were subcontractor's shanties and on floors where form work and decking was being laid. Each watchman was familiar with the working of the water supply system as described under the heading of Temporary Water for Utility and Fire Protection.

TEMPORARY WATER SYSTEM FOR UTILITY PURPOSES AND
FIRE PROTECTION

Temporary Risers and Waste Lines:

Keeping pace with the erection of the structural steel, a 3" riser was installed from the 2nd Basement to the 30th Floor and a 4" riser from the 2nd Basement to the 85th floor.

Both risers at every floor were equipped with two 3/4" L.K. valve connections and on every other floor a 2½" valve connection was installed on a 4" riser to which a fire hose could be attached in case of emergency.

A 4" temporary waste line was provided for each riser mentioned above, connecting to a sewer in the basement.

A full-sized watertight barrel was placed at each riser on every floor and a 2" branch connected each water barrel to the 4" waste line to take care of the overflow.

Two Temporary Wooden Tanks Used:

A temporary 4,000 gallon cypress tank was first set up on the 21st floor and as soon as the steel structure had been erected high enough to permit, this same tank was removed and placed on the 42nd floor, where it remained for the construction period.

The second tank, which was also of 4,000 gallon capacity, cypress and was first set up on the 63d floor was later moved up to the 85th floor for the duration of the work.

Pumping System for Temporary Water Supply:

In the First Basement, four pumps, each size 4"x3" - 15 H.P. were installed to pump the water through 3" and 4" risers to fill the tank which was first located on the 21st floor and later on the 42nd floor. Connections into the top and bottom of the tank, with proper checks and valves, were installed in order to allow the 4" riser to be used for filling the tank with water, as well as feeding the water down from the tank.

An automatic float switch on the temporary tank on the 42nd floor operated a gong signal to notify the pumpmen in the First Basement Pumproom when it was necessary to start the pumps to fill the tank to the proper level.

On the 41st floor were located three pumps; two were 2½"x 2"- 5 H.P. and one large pump was 4" - 100 H.P. used for boosting the water from the tank on the 42nd floor up to the 63d floor tank and later to the 85th floor tank.

On the 84th floor, one pump was installed, size 3" x 2" - 10 H.P. and this pump was used for pumping water from the 85th floor tank up to the top of the mooring mast through a 2½" riser. 2½" valve connections were made at each floor in the mooring mast section from this 2½" temporary riser, which supplied water for building purposes and also allowed use of a 2½" fire hose in case of fire emergency.

Automatic float switches on the tanks signalled down to the pumproom when the water level receded to a point where all pumps had to be started to refill the tanks to working capacity.

Temporary wooden Water Tank -
4000 gals. - 20th floor.

A temporary water supply is required during construc-
tion to feed the temporary toilets, for on-site restaurant
kitchens, temporary fire-protection service, and the "wet
trades": concrete, masonry, and plaster. Pressure from
the city mains in New York will lift water only to the
fifth- or sixth-floor level. Just as most tall buildings have
a permanent water tank at the top to supply water down,
two temporary tanks were used for the temporary supply.
This photograph shows the first tank when it was on the
20th floor. (#207 7/18/30)

Main Permanent Standpipe Tied Into Temporary Water System:

The No.1 Standpipe which is 8" in diameter, extends from the street siamese connections up to the 83d floor.

In order to have immediately available at all times, a sufficient supply of water for fire-fighting purposes without waiting for the city fire engines to arrive to hook up to the street siamese connections for No.1 standpipe, this main standpipe was connected up with the temporary water system. By opening a special valve on the 41st floor and starting the large 4" - 100 HP pump on that floor, this standpipe immediately became wet and available for use, with an outlet valve and 200 feet of 2½" fire hose on every floor.

Five additional 8" standpipes which were kept dry, extend from the siamese connections on the three streets up to the 20th floor and are immediately available for hook-up by the city fire engines.

Pumpman - Electrician - Hoisting Engineer, Always on Duty:

To take care of any fire which might occur a 24-hour day service is maintained whereby a pumpman is always on hand to supply water - an electrician to supply necessary light and power - and a hoisting engineer to operate an emergency hoist or elevator for lifting firemen up to the floor upon which a fire might break out.

The above mentioned maintenance men, as well as our night and day watchmen are thoroughly instructed and form the main personnel of our fire-fighting organization.

Each day an inspection is made by different firemen from the local fire headquarters in order that their entire company will be thoroughly familiar with the construction of the building and the facilities available for fighting a fire.

Temporary Toilets for Use of Workmen:

As a part of the temporary plumbing work, it was necessary to construct temporary toilets for the use of the workmen. These toilets were of cast iron construction, each 12 feet long and of the type known as school sinks.

The toilets were erected on every fourth floor from the 2nd basement to the 23d floor inclusive, and on every sixth floor above the 23d floor level.

85 stories of steel complete.

This overall shot, taken as the main steel framing was topped out, shows the effect of the extensive use of interior hoists. Only a few cranes are visible, unlike most tall building construction sites of the 1920s and '30s. Ordinary construction methods used at the time would have incorporated a set of cranes for the steel, a set for bulk materials such as brick or gypsum, and a set for the façade panels and windows. The interior hoists allowed for hoisting the bulk and façade materials with little interference from the weather, and more important, with little of the cross-interference sometimes created by the different sets of cranes. (#281 9/20/30)

Hoisting flag at "topping off steel" on 86th floor.

The ancient European tradition of tieing a fir tree to the top of a newly completed roof lives on among American steelworkers. Either a small tree or a flag is tied to the completed frame when it reaches its top. At the Empire State, the first topping out ceremony was photographed when the main building frame was completed at the 86th floor. (#273 3:30 PM 9/19/30)

THE FASCINATION OF SPEED

During the course of the construction work, visitors appeared, who were representative of every continent, and practically every civilized country. Architects and Civil Engineers from Europe, Mechanical Engineers from China, Japan and Russia and Builders from South Africa , Australia, New Zealand and South America.

From Canada and various parts of the United States, many men visiting the City, who had an interest in building construction or any of its allied activities, were anxious to visit the building.

Students from foreign universities, traveling under the auspices of the International Student Federation, and classes from practically every large technical school or college within the territory bounded by Boston, Ithaca and Washington, D.C. paid a visit to the newest giant of skyscrapers in the making.

This varied assortment of visitors tended to confirm our belief that New York City is the cosmopolitan hub of the World.

Inquisitive sightseers who were merely anxious to go to the top just to get the view and satisfy their curiosity, were legion and of course they had to be discouraged. They were urged to wait until the finished building, with its special observation galleries in the mooring mast section, would afford them the pleasure they sought under safer and more comfortable circumstances.

The former class of people, who had legitimate reasons and proper credentials for visiting the building were for the most part familiar with the American Skyscraper and this building was one higher than all the rest. They had heard about the economical factors responsible for the popularity of this type of building, especially on Manhattan Island. They knew of some of the aggrevation a building of this size would create, in relation to the traffic problem. Many did not hesitate to criticize the super-skyscraper as being an exaggeration that was unnecessary and expressed doubt as to its financial success.

There was one feature of the enterprise, however, that caused every one to marvel and that amazing feature was the short space of time alloted for its erection.

The first steel columns were set on April 7th, 1930 and the building had to be completed and ready for occupancy May 1st, 1931 - practically one year after the start of the steel erection. A building 85 stories high surmounted by a 200 ft. mooring mast - bringing the total height of the structure to 1,252 feet.

As a rule, this information was received increduously, especially by foreigners, and when the truth became apparent, it was pronounced marvelous that the enormous quantities of material and equipment needed could be fabricated, shipped from the various sources - in many cases from foreign countries - and erected into a complete structure within the short space of time of one year.

The information was generally volunteered that a similar project in one of the older countries would take many years to build.

View of lot from 5th Ave. elevation.

This overall view from the southeast shows the site ready for steel erection to begin. The large cranes standing upright were used at the lower levels for picking up steel from trucks and setting it in place. (#47 4/5/30)

Col. forms clamped and reinforcing bars for basement Retaining Wall.

The columns in the basement levels were fireproofed by being encased in concrete. This photograph shows the wood forms surrounding a steel column in front of rebar being placed for an exterior basement wall. (#109 5/13/30)

THE FOUR PACEMAKERS

In considering the factor of speed, it is interesting to study the progress of those four divisions of the construction work which had to take the lead and set the pace for other trades that followed.

These four leaders in the order of their sequence were:

1. Structural Steel Erection
2. Concrete Floor Arch Construction
3. Exterior Metal Trim and Aluminum Spandrels (including metal windows)
4. Exterior Limestone (exterior trim and limestone backed up with common brick)

Structural Steel:

The structural steel for the eighty-five stories of the Main Building was topped out on September 19th, 1930 and completely set on September 22,1930.

The progress schedule called for completion of the steel on Oct.4,1930.

The time gained was twelve days.

Concrete Floor Arch Construction:

The floors for 85 stories including the Main Roof at the 86th floor level were completely poured on October 6, 1930.

The progress schedule called for completion of floor arches on Oct.10,1930.

The time gained was four days.

Exterior Metal Trim and Cast Aluminum Spandrels:

This work for the 85 stories was completely erected on October 17,1930. The progress schedule set Dec. 1,1930 as the completion date. The time-saving effected was 35 days.

Exterior Limestone (Including Common Brick Backup):

The 85 stories were completely enclosed on Nov.13,1930 ; a gain of 17 days over the schedule completion date of Dec.1,1930.

Revision of Progress Schedule:

The impetus gained by the various other trades following closely on the trail of the four leaders mentioned above, permitted a change to be made in the progress schedule. The original progress schedule called for completion of the construction work on April 1, 1931 in order to allow tenants to move in and start occupancy on May 1, 1931. The success achieved in being able to completely enclose the building before the advent of severe weather, permitted the final completion date to be advanced one month to March 1, 1931.

Hoisting column from 33rd Street.

The lower columns are made up of built-up sections, similar in concept to the pieces used in the earlier Waldorf-Astoria, but much larger. The standard sizes of rolled steel section were not adequate for the extraordinarily high loads at the base of the building, so reinforcing plates were riveted on. The top surface of the column shows one of these added plates. The small pieces of steel projecting up from it, and those projecting to the left and right, are connections for the first-tier beams. (#56 4/9/30)

Tower Foundation Columns.

Several lowest-level columns have been set on their reinforced concrete piers some thirty feet below the street. The connection plates for the beams are visible on the column faces, as is the relatively large round hole in the top of the nearest column, which is used to attach a hook, so that the column can be lifted into place by a crane. (#50 4/7/30)

6. STRUCTURAL STEEL

THE CHIEF facts covering the structural steel can be summarized as follows:

1. Order for furnishing and erecting steel was given to Post & McCord, January 2, 1930

2. First information on steel design supplied January 15, 1930

3. All steel made by Carnegie Steel Company and fabricated by American Bridge Company and the McClintic-Marshall Company, subsidiaries of the United States Steel Corporation

4. Steel shipped from the shops as fast as fabricated and stored in the Pennsylvania Railroad yards at Greenville, N.J. From that place the steel was lightered to wharf on North River and trucked to the site as required

5. Real start of erection on April 1st, 1930

6. Steel for roof (85th floor) set by September 22, 1930

7. Elapse of time, 25 weeks for the erection of 87 stories (including two basements)

8. Tonnage erected on September 22nd, 1930, 57,480 tons

9. Greatest number of men employed on steel erection 350

Size of Task Involved:

The placing of more than 57,480 tons of structural steel in an eighty five story building between the months of April and October was the difficult task that confronted Post & McCord, Incorporated - the contractors who furnished and erected the structural steel.

Eighty percent of this total tonnage was in place on August first, when the building had reached to about the 50th story. During July, 22 stories of steel were placed in 22 working days, involving regular hours and no night work. Progress averaged about 10,000 tons per month for the erection of the entire 57,480 tons. A five-day week prevailed throughout the erection period.

Comparison with other Large Erection Contracts:

The steel tonnage in the Empire State Building exceeds by a large margin that used in any comparable structure. The Chrysler Building utilized 21,000 tons and the 70-story Manhattan Company Building in New York City required 18,500 tons. The Merchandize Mart in Chicago, recently characterized as the world's largest building, required only 38,000 tons. The principal roof of the Empire State Building is 1045'4" above the curb, with a combination airship mooring mast and observation tower 206'8" above this point, to a total height of 1252 feet. The building's completed height will exceed that of the Chrysler Building - now the tallest structure, by something over 200 feet.

Setting Col. 115 - 72,795 lbs. (on right is largest)
Col. #105 - 102,830 lbs. 14″ x 26′8″ x 13′ base.

One of the columns is suspended by a crane and is being slowly pushed into position above its pier. The small pieces of steel projecting up from the pier (by the legs of the iron worker) are attached to the steel grillage set within the pier and serve as guides for correct placement. (#65 4/11/30)

STRUCTURAL STEEL - Continued

The following detailed account of the erection of the structural steel was prepared by Post & McCord and was printed in Engineering News Record, August 1, 1930:

280   ENGINEERING NEWS-RECORD   *August 21, 1930*

Planning and Control Permit Erection of 85 Stories of Steel in Six Months

Empire State Building in New York City Involving 57,000 Tons Goes Up in Record Time—Nine Derricks Starting Work on 425x198-Ft. Site Reduced to Five Above Twentieth Floor—Relay Platforms Necessary in Hoisting Steel—All Hoists Inside of Building

FIG. 1—EMPIRE STATE BUILD-ING, NEW YORK CITY

THE PLACING of more than 57,000 tons of structural steel in an 85-story building between the months of April and October is the task which has confronted the steel erector on the Empire State Building in New York City. Eighty per cent of this total tonnage was in place on Aug. 1, when the building had reached to about the 50th story. During July, 22 stories of steel were placed in 22 working days, involving regular hours and no night work. As progress has averaged about 10,000 tons of steel per month (working five days a week), it seems probable that the difficult schedule will be met.

This article is devoted to an account of the steel erector's methods and equipment which are of interest and value both because of the magnitude of the project and the careful planning and control which has been exercised. The steel tonnage in the Empire State Building exceeds by a large margin that used in any comparable structure. The Chrysler Building utilized 21,000 tons and the 70-story Manhattan Company Building, both in New York City, required 18,500 tons. The Merchandise Mart in Chicago, recently characterized as the world's largest building, required only 38,000 tons. The principal roof of the Empire State Building is 1,043 ft. above the curb, and latest plans contemplate the addition of a combination airship mooring mast and observation tower approximately 200 ft. tall above this point. The building's completed height will exceed that of the Chrysler Building, now the tallest structure, by something over 200 feet.

In preparing a plan of procedure for the steel erection, it was necessary to consider four major problems: (1) steel supply, which had to take into account the fabrication schedule and methods of delivery; (2) plant layout, including number, size and location of derricks and hoisting engines; (3) steel-handling methods at the job, which necessarily had to be considered as complementary to plant layout in the planning; and (4) actual erection procedure, including methods of setting, fitting up and riveting.

Steel Supply

The large tonnage in the building and the urgency for completion made it advisable to divide the fabricating contract between two firms, the American Bridge Co. and the McClintic-Marshall Co. Alternate sections from the basement to the roof, comprising from two to eight floors each, were assigned to each fabricator. All steel is shipped to a joint waterfront supply yard near Bayonne, N. J., and steel for erection is ordered from this supply yard one lift (two floors) at a time, as needed. Because of possible delays in loading and shipment it is necessary for the steel erector to order steel two days in advance of the time it is to be used. Since there is no storage space at the building site, it is absolutely necessary that everything be in readiness to erect the steel when it arrives.

Steel is delivered from the supply yard to docks on the East River waterfront by derrick-equipped lighters. Columns and heavy members are transferred to trucks at 23d St. while the smaller material comes ashore at 19th St. Since the Empire State Building is between 33d and 34th St. on Fifth Ave., the haul through city streets is not long. The largest shipping pieces were the two bottom column sections, the lower one 15 ft. 8 in. long, weighing 44 tons, and the upper one having about the same weight but being 33 ft. long. By using a two-wheel trailer, the trucks were able to handle these sections as easily as the smaller ones.

At the beginning of the job steel was delivered to the 33d St. side of the building; an unusually wide sidewalk on 34th St. made it impossible for the derricks standing in the excavation to reach trucks on this side. When erection had reached the second floor, however, the derricks could reach either street and steel was delivered on both the 33d and 34th St. sides until erection reached the 46th floor, when unloading on 34th St. was discontinued. All steel is now being received along 33d St. which, although narrow, is a westbound street permitting the trucks to reach the building from the East River waterfront in the most direct manner.

The erection plant is divided into two main parts—

FIG. 2—EARLY ERECTION VIEW OF EMPIRE STATE BUILDING

At stage shown almost 8,000 tons of steel had been erected. Note extent of site which is 198x425 ft. General contractors' offices on bridge over 5th Ave. in foreground. Note complete planking of top floor forming a safe working platform for the steel erectors. Also at left, trucks unloading steel and materials along 33rd St. side.

Slab forms with mesh and conduit - 2nd floor.

The floor slabs are concrete, which was placed so that it simultaneously formed the slabs and encasement around the floor beams. The horizontal lines interrupting the wood forms in the photograph are the floor beams; the grid on top of the beams and the forms is the wire mesh that reinforces the slab. The two rolls on the left are unused mesh. The heavy vertical line left of center is electrical conduit to be embedded in the slab when the concrete was placed. (#96 5/7/30)

Running conduit over mesh on slab forms of 2nd floor.

An electrician installs conduit after the mesh has been placed. (#97 5/7/30)

Concreting the 6th floor set-back. Capacity of Concrete Buggies - 6 cu. ft.

The man on the right delivers concrete from a buggy with a six-cubic-yard capacity, enough to create twelve to fifteen square feet of floor. The men on the left stand in the wet concrete, spreading it into position, pushing it into the wood forms around the beams that create the beam encasement, and mixing it to keep cement from rising to the top and the aggregate from settling to the bottom. (#114 5/22/30)

2nd floor concrete slab set 24 hours.

Within a day concrete sets up hard enough to support a person's weight. This slab is only one day old; it is set, but would still have been supported by form-work for at least another three or four days. (#99 5/9/30)

Stripping concrete slab and soffit forms. "Arch Forms"

After the concrete had hardened and gained enough strength to support its own weight, the wood forms below were removed. Here the slab and beam encasement forms are being removed. (#171 7/9/30)

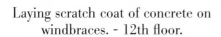

Laying scratch coat of concrete on windbraces. - 12th floor.

Above grade, the columns were fireproofed with terra-cotta tile and the beams were fireproofed with cast-in-place concrete encasement. The large diagonal wind braces that give the building its lateral strength could not easily be fireproofed using either method. Cementitious fireproofing was applied to wire lath fastened to a brace. (#192 7/15/30)

CONCRETE FLOOR ARCHES AND GENERAL CONCRETE
FIREPROOFING

Concrete Floor Arches:

Throughout the 85-story Main Building, 4" cinder concrete floor arches were used (1:2:5 mix) and these were reinforced with galvanized welded fabric 3x16 - 6x10.

Over 62,000 cubic yards of concrete was placed in these arches.

The wire mesh reinforcement was used to the extent of 2,900,00 sq.ft.

Beam and girder reinforcement clips covered 700,000 lineal feet of beam and girder soffits.

Slab forms for arches were placed over an area of 1,900,000 sq.ft.

The beam and girder side and soffit forms covered an area of 2,225,000 square feet.

Concrete Fireproofing of Columns:

A stone concrete fireproofing was poured around all sub-basement columns four inches thick for exterior columns and 2" thick for interior columns.

Stone concrete fireproofing, four inches thick was used around exterior basement columns along the west property line.

Cinder concrete fireproofing was used for all other basement columns and all columns through the first floor to the extent of four inches in thickness on exterior columns and two inches in thickness on interior columns.

This work in place developed the fact that 125,000 square feet of forms had been used for columns; 120,000 square feet of wire mesh for column wrapping reinforcement and 2,000 cubic yards of concrete.

Fireproofing Steel Windbraces:

From the second Basement to the 86th floor roof, special wind bracing for the steel structure extended up through the Main Tower Area.

This windbracing was covered with Clinton wire cloth upon which two inches of cement fireproofing was applied.

This work involved the covering of an area of 91,000 square feet with Clinton wire mesh and cement fireproofing.

All of the concrete work (except for floor fill and finish) was done by the Builders.

Setting stone with "Horton" lewis - 8th floor.

Two masons are setting a piece of the exterior stone, hung from a winch, into place between two vertical stainless steel mullions. The ornamented panel on the left is a cast aluminum panel, which will later have a window placed above it. (#155 6/18/30)

Backing up Stainless Steel, Metal Trim and Cast Aluminum Spandrel with common brick.

In 1930 the building code still required masonry fireproofing of exterior walls, even when the walls did not require masonry for support. The brick piers are fireproofing for the stainless steel mullions. The mullions carry all of the wind and gravity load of the windows and limestone piers, while the code-required brick prevents interior fires from damaging the wall. (#306 9/24/30)

EXTERIOR METAL SPANDRELS AND TRIM

Over 300 tons of Chrome-nickle steel, most commonly known as 18-8, was used on the exterior of the building for the window trim, mullions and ornamental window heads.

Almost 300 tons of cast aluminum spandrels were also used on the exterior of the building.

The chrome-nickle corrosion-resisting steel contains 17-20% chromium, 7-10% nickle, less than 0.20% carbon, less than 0.50% manganese, over 0.50% silicon, and maximum of 0.025% sulplur and phosphorus.

The alloy is Austenitic in structure, that is, all the carbon is in solution and in that condition it is rust-resisting in a moist atmosphere , even in salt air.

This alloy metal is coming rapidly into use as a building material but the Empire State Building has had more extensive treatment with this metal than any other building up to the present time.

Where Metal is Used on Building:

The vertical lines of polished steel begin at the sixth floor and extend upward for the full height, merging at the top in great sunbursts at the window heads. It is again used in the mooring mast to the extent of 25 tons.

Window openings are arranged in groups of twos and threes - the groups separated by limestone piers.

At the sides of each window group is a trim of the chrome-nickle steel, 10 inches wide and the windows of the same group are separated by mullions of the alloy, 22 inches wide.

The plane of both these metal sections is broken by vertical angles carefully worked out to give the desired light and shade, the lines of these angles extending vertically the full 85 stories above the fifth floor and broken only by the setbacks.

The dark vertical lines of the windows are kept intact by use of the cast aluminum spandrels, the dark gray of which merge with the window black.

Back view of first tier of Limestone on 2nd floor showing
anchors mortared in stone.

The second-floor exterior wall is under construction. The hanging scaffold on the outside of the building in front of the bungalows is used for setting the exterior stone, while the back-up brick masonry is built from the interior floor. (#213 9/24/30)

EXTERIOR METAL SPANDRELS AND TRIM - Continued

Manufacturers of Chrome-Nickle Steel:

Half of the steel was supplied by the Republic Steel Corporation of Massilon, Ohio and the other half by the Allegheny Steel Company of Brackenridge, Pa.

The cast aluminum spandrels were supplied by the Aluminum Company of America of Cleveland, Ohio.

Fabricators:

The contract for fabricating the 6,352 pieces of window trim and 2,752 mullions - making a total of 9,105 sections (or a total of over twenty miles if laid end to end) was awarded to the United Metal Products Co. of Canton, Ohio.

The trim and mullions are made of 18 gauge, although some 16 and 22 gauge stock was made for reinforcement purposes. The longest section fabricated was 151 9/16 inches - a typical section, 139 9/16 inches.

Fabrication operations included a limited amount of punching of the corners of the sheets, bending or forming, spot and seam welding and polishing of the welded points.

Each metal unit is reinforced with 18-8 channel strips at intervals of about two feet.

The reinforcing channel strips; anchor strips; interlocking clips or backing strips and 2x2x¼ inch structural steel angles 12 inches long, two at each end of every section, are electric spot welded to the chrome-nickle sections.

Method of Attaching to Structure:

The facing is fastened to the structural steel of the building at the floor levels with web plates and structural brackets.

Additional anchorage is provided between floors by strap anchors set in the brick work and bolted to the reinforcing channel strips. Bolts of 1/2 and 3/4 inch diameter are used in anchoring.

The sections fit together with a lap joint occurring at each floor level thereby providing for the contraction and expansion of the metal. The lap joint is sealed with a continuous interlocking clip at each joint to make the connection weathertight.

Mooring Mast deckplate finished and caulked.

The mooring mast appears from a distance to have a rounded top, but it actually is a truncated dome. The flat deck in this picture is the very top of the mast—the highest point on the building before the construction of the radio antenna—in addition to being the intended anchor point for dirigibles. (#538 3/18/30)

South side of Mooring Mast FF to HH level or (102nd floor)

Seen at close range, the top half of the mooring mast is a complicated geometry executed in stainless steel. Hidden by the base of the mast from visitors on the 86th floor, as well as from the 102nd floor observation deck, the faceted shaft contributes to the long-range visual effect. (#547 3/21/30)

EXTERIOR METAL SPANDRELS AND TRIM - Continued

Handling and Shipping to Job:

Extreme care had to be exercised in handling the sections after the
final polishing operations had been completed. Polished surfaces
must not be allowed to come in contact with any object which might
scratch and cause opportunity for corrosion.

In shipping the finished sections to New York, the United Metal
Products Company used cardboard cartons. To prevent the stacked
cartons from aggregating too heavy a dead load on those cartons in
the bottom of the car and to prevent shifting, a framework of wood
was erected and the cartons supported in sections. These sections
were unloaded intact from the cars and placed on trucks for transportation to the building.

Erection Sub-Contractors:

Two subcontractors erected the metal - each being assigned two
adjacent sides of the building and their work progressed concurrently.

C.E.Halback and Company and William H.Jackson Company, both of Brooklyn,
New York did the erection work.

The combined forces of both of these subcontractors on the date of
greatest activity numbered ninety men.

Swinging Limestone column section
into place. - 5th Ave. Entrance.

*Some of the most heavily carved and orna-
mented limestone is at the base of the building,
especially surrounding the entrances. The large
piece of stone being placed is a portion of one
of the ornamental columns flanking the Fifth
Avenue entrance. (#303 10/2/30)*

Setting Swedish Black Granite decoration blocks over 5th Ave. entrance.

*Almost all of the façade veneer is limestone. Here decorative black granite for the Fifth
Avenue entrance is being set in the same manner as the other decorative stone. (#283
9/23/30)*

EXTERIOR LIMESTONE

Contract for Furnishing Stone:

Prior to requests for estimates from the local stone contractors, the concensus of opinion in the stone trade was that the stonework required for the Empire State Building would amount to the largest quantity of cubic feet of stone ever required for a building operation in the Metropolitan District.

As a matter of fact, the final treatment of the exterior of the building called for 198,328 cubic feet of limestone which is considerably less than the 377,222 cubic feet of limestone used in the New York Life Building - the nearest comparable building in the use of exterior limestone.

The stonework for the New York Life Building was much heavier in cubic feet, because it was more ornamental, with all jambs 1'8" deep and heavy window arches and piers.

On account of the extensive use of the exterior metal trim and spandrels on the Empire State Building, the stone work was much simplified. Practically 80% of the stonework consisted of piers of three pieces of stone, 4" deep and one piece 8" deep, each pier for each story.

The contract for furnishing the stone was awarded to William Bradley and Son and Three associates, on the following basis:

William Bradley and Son	54,126' 10" cu. ft.
B.A. and C.N. Williams	54,126' 10" " "
J.J. Spurr & Son	51,987' 3" " "
J. Gillies & Son	38,087' 1" " "
	198,328' 0" " "

Rough Stock:

Rough stock was bought from the Indiana Limestone Company of Bedford, Indiana and the records show that there were delivered, 205,383'0" cubic feet of sawed slabs and blocks, which required 369 cars to deliver to the various plants. This shows less than 4% waste. To expedite the completion of the stone cutting, The Indiana Limestone Company sawed a large portion of the stone at their mills; quarried special sizes so that the slabs would come to the planers in sizes convenient to make two pieces each for the larger piers and satisfied the plants, generally, in the quantity and quality of the stock shipped.

Stone Cutting:

All the cutting was practically completed at the local plants early in September 1930 and deliveries to the job from these plants were satisfactory to the extent that we believe a record for erection of stonework has been established on this building.

Heavy Limestone blocks on flatcar - 1st floor.

The limestone blocks used in the façade are among the heavier and the more fragile nonstructural elements used in the building. The blocks were carried on large flat cars to prevent damage during movement within the building. (#229 8/6/30)

Limestone Block (3 1/2 tons) to be raised to 85th floor.

Most of the limestone used in the façade is a relatively thin veneer, but in areas of carved ornamentation, thicker pieces of stone were required. This block, weighing 3 1/2 tons, is at the 85th floor, where cut stone ornament decorates the edges of the top setbacks below the main roof. (#349 10/30/30)

EXTERIOR LIMESTONE - Continued

Stone Setting:

The stone was set by the General Contractor. Setting began on June
fifth, 1930 and was completed on November 13, 1930 - during a total
of 113 working days.   The only stonework remaining to be done at
that time was in a few places where derricks were placed for mooring
mast construction and the stone work could not be put in place until
a later date.

After the erection work reached its full swing, we believe all records
for stonesetting heretofore held were broken during the progress of the
work.

The stonesetting was started at the 6th floor setback and the rate of
speed averaged one floor a day after the force was thoroughly organized.

A study made of the limestone set from Monday, September 8, 1930 to
Friday September 19,1930, inclusive, or in ten working days, disclosed
the fact that during that period 14 1/7 stories of limestone had been
set.

Method of Unloading and Raising Stone:

The methods of unloading and distributing this exterior limestone as
described in a previous chapter, were an innovation in this territory
and, no doubt, were responsible in a large measure for the satisfactory
speed of setting maintained.

All of the limestone was unloaded from trucks inside the building on
the Main Floor with the aid of an overhead mono-rail trolley system.
The stone was placed on platform cars, pushed onto material hoists,
raised to the required floor and distributed with the aid of industrial
track on each floor to its proper location.

A few large pieces had to be raised by a steel derrick to the 85th
story for setting at this level.

All limestone for the lower part of the building up to and including
the fifth story was raised by stiff-leg derricks placed on the sixth
floor setback and lowered from that point for setting by Sasgen stiff
leg derricks.

Eagle head being set atop South Column of
5th Avenue Entrance

*The tops of the decorative columns flanking the building
entrances are carved stone eagles. The padded ropes lead to
a stone winch, which supports the large block as the masons
maneuver it into place. (#338 10/22/30)*

<u>LIMESTONE</u> - Continued

<u>Cowing Pressure Relieving Joint</u>:

Cowing pressure relieving joints were used in connection with the stone setting as shown in the illustration.

<u>Description and Purpose</u>:

This joint was invented and perfected to overcome the serious problem of cracked and spalled facing blocks which have marred so many beautiful buildings.

The joint consists of a corrugated sheet lead filler enclosed in a sheet lead envelope - the thickness of the bed joint. It is usually installed across the piers and intermediate pilasters in lieu of one mortar joint to each story.

When used in this manner the joint zones the facade and prevents the breaking or spalling of stone facing blocks due to any of the following causes ; (a) shortening of steel, caused by seasonal temperature changes, (b) compression of steel due to load of the building and its contents, (c) sudden temperature changes which expand or contract the face of the building without reaching the inner columns, (d) wind stresses, (e) vibration and (f) settlement.

It is a known fact that a steel column twenty feet high, when loaded to 16,000 lbs. per square inch will be nearly 1/8 inch shorter than before the load was applied, the shelf angles in the upper stories, instead of supporting the ashlar, may rest on the stone below and automatically transfer the weight of the structure to the ashlar. As buildings have become higher and masonry units larger, the provision of joints of a semi-plastic nature have become increasingly important.

These joints cut to proper sizes were supplied by the Cowing Pressure Relieving Joint Company of Chicago, through their New York Representative, the Fireproof Products Company, Incorporated.

ELEVATORS

We must keep in mind that the eighty-five stories of the building surmounted by a mooring mast tower, rises to a total height of 1,252 feet above the street level. Commensurate with this unprecedented height, the cubical contents of the building is nearly 36,000,00 cu.ft.

Planning the elevator service for a building of these proportions is a special problem necessitating a thorough study of the requirements by competent engineers. Adequate elevator service must be provided to all floors, since the rental value of a floor depends largely upon the character of the elevator service which is provided.

With a building of this height, the problem of securing the necessary elevator service with the least possible encroachment on the net rental area is especially important. Its solution in this case was the selection of high-speed elevators having the most efficient and time-saving method of operation obtainable. This permitted the specifying of the fewest number of elevators for the maximum service required.

Plan of Elevator Lobby

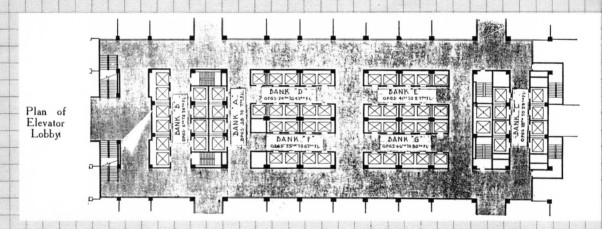

From: "The Empire State Building. VIII. Elevators" by Jones, Bassett in *Architectural Forum* 54 (January 1931) 97.

ELEVATORS - Continued

Main Passenger Elevators

The fifty-eight main passenger elevators are grouped in seven banks, centrally located in the building. With the exception of Bank A, all of the elevators have express zones as indicated in the summary shown later. It will be noted in this summary, that the stops of the various groups overlap to provide "exchange" floors for inter-floor traffic and flexibility in the arrangement of the local and express zones.

Each of these elevators is of the Otis Signal Control type, embodying Unit Multi-Voltage Control and Micro-Leveling. The operation is briefly summarized in the following paragraphs.

Operation:

The various control switches and buttons for the operation of each car are conveniently grouped in the operating panel in the car. As passengers enter the car, the attendent registers the desired floor stops by pressing corresponding buttons located in the upper section of the Car Operating Panel.

The buttons may be pressed in any sequence, either before or after the car is started, and they remain depressed until the completion of the trip.

The doors are closed and the car is started by moving the starting handle to its operating position.

After starting, the car proceeds to the first floor for which a car or hall button has been pressed. As it approaches the floor, it is automatically slowed down and stopped with the platform level with the floor sill. The car and hatch doors open automatically during the leveling of the car.

A prospective passenger in one of the upper halls is advised of the approach and direction of travel of a car stopping at the floor by the illumination of the corresponding hall lantern over the elevator entrance. Since the lantern is illuminated only for a car actually stopping at the floor, false signals are avoided. The lantern remains lighted until the car leaves the floor. The control is so designed that the first available car approaching the floor in the desired direction will stop in answer to the pressing of a hall button and will automatically cancel the call so as to prevent unnecessary stops by any other car.

Night Service

Passenger traffic at night is handled by the ten elevators of Bank "C". For this night service, elevators Nos. 3 and 4 operate locally between the ground and 19th floors inclusive; Nos. 6 and 7 operate express to the 42nd floor and locally from there to the 66th floor. The remaining four elevators of this bank operate express to the 66th floor and locally from there to the 80th floor.

ELEVATORS - Continued

Signal System

The distinct operating advantages characteristic of Otis Signal Control are supplemented with an adequate Otis Signal System in order that the traffic may be handled efficiently and with the greatest convenience to the passengers.

Hall Lanterns:

Hall lanterns are provided above all of the entrances. The lanterns are equipped with single stroke bells to give audible as well as visual indication of the approach of the cars.

Indicator Panels:

The operation of each bank of elevators is under the supervision of a starter who, by means of an Indicator Panel located on one of the lobby walls, can see where each car is, its direction of travel and at what floors there are prospective passengers. Blue Non-stop lights in the panel also show when a car, fully loaded or for some other reason, is passing floors at which it normally should stop for waiting passengers. The Indicator Panel also gives the starter complete information regarding the scheduling of the elevators.

Control Panels:

A Starter's Control Panel located on the lobby wall opposite to the Indicator Panel provides means for controlling the movement of the elevators. The panel includes buttons for signalling to the car attendants, a telephone and various switches for controlling the scheduling device.

Car Position Indicators:

Otis Horizontal Multi-light Position Indicators are located above doors in each car. Illuminated numerals in the fixtures show the attendant and the passengers the location of the car and its direction of travel.

Telephones:

A Private Automatic Exchange telephone system with a two-hundred station board provides for communication between the cars, the Starter's Control Panels, the machine rooms and the Superintendent's and Chief Engineer's offices. It also includes a telephone station in the elevator corridor on each floor.

The telephone instruments in the cars are mounted in flush-type boxes, the covers of which also serve as certificate holders.

ELEVATORS - Continued

Signal System Continued

Scheduling:

In common with a rapidly growing practice, in important buildings, each bank of passenger elevators is provided with an Otis Scheduling Device. The purpose of this equipment is to automatically dispatch the elevators and, at the same time, permit the starter to control their operation in such a manner as to secure the utmost quantity and quality of service obtainable, under the varying traffic conditions.

The dispatching is accomplished by means of lights located in each Car Operating Panel. One of these lights indicates to the attendant in a car when his car is the next one to leave a terminal. Other lights indicate when he is to start the car.

At the terminal landing, prospective passengers are advised of the next car to leave by the illumination of the hall lantern above the entrance to this car.

Provision is made for dispatching the cars from either or both terminals in the order of their arrival, or from both terminals in a predetermined sequence. Lights in the Starter's Indicator Panel enable the starter to determine whether or not the car attendants are complying with the dispatching signals.

Freight Elevators:

All of the freight elevators (with the exception of the two low-rise cars Nos. 5 and 6, which have target annunciators) are provided with the flashlight annunciators. They are also equipped with dial indicators at all floors. Because of the great number of floors served by cars Nos. 1 to 4 inclusive, the dial indicators for these elevators are furnished with numerals for every tenth floor only.

Fixtures:

All car and corridor fixtures in the signal system of the main passenger elevators are cast of special aluminum in Otis foundries.

ELEVATORS - Continued

Doors

There are a total of 1239 elevator entrances, all of which (with the exception of six metal clad counterbalanced freight doors) are of the single-speed center-opening type. The doors for the main passenger elevators are built especially for high speed power operation.

The 58 first-floor doors are of modern design in three colors and are constructed of natural bronze, aluminum and enameled steel. The 1175 upper floor doors are of steel, flush panel type with baked enamel finish.

The car doors of the main passenger elevators are of the solid, single-speed center-opening type. Otis tubular type safety gates are used on the freight elevators and the two tower elevators.

Door Operation

Each of the main passenger elevators is equipped with an Otis High Speed Electric Door Operator, which automatically opens the hatchway and car doors as the car is stopping at a floor. The doors are closed by spring pressure when the attendant initiates the starting of the car, and are liquid checked, in both directions of travel. The speed of operation is adjustable so that advantage can be taken of a higher speed for opening than for closing.

Interlocks are provided which prevent moving the elevator away from a landing unless all doors are closed and locked. The movement of the doors is synchronized with the micro-leveling of the car so that they are open by the time the car platform is level with the sill. This facilitates the transfer of passengers. All doors can be manually operated in case of an emergency.

The doors on the freight and tower elevators and the night service openings of the main passenger elevators are equipped with Otis manual door closers.

ELEVATORS - Continued

Summary of Elevators

Passenger Elevators   Duty

Bank A, 4-Local   4000 lbs. @ 700 F.P.M.
  "   B, 10-Express   4000 "   " 700 "   (arranged for future)
  "   C, 8-Express   3500 "   " 700 "   speed of 800 F.P.M.)
  "   D, 10-Express   3500 "   " 700 "   (arranged for future
  "   E, 8-Express   3500 "   " 700 "   speed of 1000 F.P.M)
  "   F, 8-Express   3500 "   " 700 "   (arranged for future
  "   G, 10-Express   3500 "   " 700 "   speed of 1200 F.P.M.)
   (Total 58)

2 Tower Elevators   3000 lbs. " 500 F.P.M.
1 Mooring Mast Elev. 2000 "   " 500 F.P.M.

Freight Elevators   Duty

No. 1.   3500 lbs. @ 700 F.P.M.
   2.   3500 "   @ 700 F.P.M.
   3 and 4,   3500 "   @ 700 F.P.M.
   5 and 6,   5000 "   @ 250 F.P.M.

Floors Served	Rise	Operation	Platform Sizes (clear)
Sub-Basement -7th, incl.	123'1"	Signal Control	6'6"x6'11½"
Ground, 6th-20th, "	238'1"	" "	6'6"x6'11½"
Ground, 18th-25th, "	300'7"		6'6"x6'3½"
Ground, 24th-43d, "	514'1"		7'2" x 5'5"
Ground, 41st-57th, "	682'1"		7'2" x 5'5"
Ground, 56th-67th, "	799'7"		7'2" x 5'5"
Ground, 66th-80th, "	951'0"		7'2" x 5'5"
79th-86th incl.	103'3"	(Car switch UMV -)	7'0" x 5'5¾"
85th-GG Level, incl.	183'10½"	(with Micro-Leveling)	6'0" x 5'0"

Floors Served	Rise	Operation	Platform sizes (clear)
Sub-bsmnt.,Bsmnt.2nd-80th inc.	986'	(Car Switch UMV)	6'11¼" x 5'6"
" " 2nd-57th incl.	716'7"	(with Micro-)	7'2" x 5'6"
" " 2nd-25th incl.	335'	(Leveling)	6'6" x6'1"
Sub-bsmnt, Bsmnt,Ground	36'2"	Car switch resistance	6'11¼"x6'1¾"

ELEVATORS - Continued

Interesting Facts Concerning the Elevators

Elevator schedules provide for transporting 15,000 persons from the offices to the ground floor of the building between 5;00 and 5:30 P.M. daily.

Nearly 8,000,000 feet - or over 1515 miles of rubber-covered wire and 190,000 feet - or nearly 36 miles of conduit are utilized in the elevator installation.

The total length of elevator hoisting ropes, compensating ropes and governor ropes is 636,361 feet - or over 120 miles.

The main and counterweight rails for the elevators total 143,272 feet - or about 27 miles.

Freight elevator No. 1, with a rise of 986 feet has the greatest travel of any of the elevators. This elevator serves a total of 81 openings.

ELEVATOR DOORS

The elevator doors were furnished and installed by the Dahlstrom Metallic Door COmpany, whose executive offices and factories are at Jamestown, New York.

Quantities of Materials Used:

700,000 lbs.	of	sheet steel stock
50,000 "	"	strip steel stock
250,000 "	"	structural steel angles
10,000 "	"	Nicalum sills
170,000 "	"	Feralun sills
110,000 "	"	steel in the fabrication of tracks and hangers

Other Interesting Facts:

836 typical floor hatchway entrances were equipped for power operation

339 typical floor hatchway entrances were equipped for manual or semi-automatic operation

1,175 total hatchway entrances on 87 floors of the main building

The above hatchway entrances are arranged in seven banks for a total of 66 elevators.

The Mooring Mast Tower has seven additional swing-type hatchway entrances and four additional center-opening slide hatchway entrances.

In addition to the above, there are 58 bronze hatchway entrances for the first floor openings. The doors and jambs for these 58 first floor entrances are being furnished by the General Bronze Corporation.

Each of the main passenger, power-operated door hatchway entrances, is equipped with Otis High Speed Elevator Door Operators, which automatically open the hatchway and car doors as the car stops at each floor. These door operating mechanisms are adjustable so that a higher or slower speed operation can be maintained. Also, different speeds for opening than for closing can be obtained. The movement of the doors is synchronized with the Micro-Leveling of the car, so that the doors are in open position by the time the car platform is level with the sill. This allows for a minimum loss of time in loading and unloading passengers.

PERMANENT ELECTRICAL INSTALLATION

It is seldom that one is able to receive an accurate word description of how work is put into place on a building operation from the man directly in charge of the work. We asked Bill McCrom, who is in charge of installing the Electrical work, to tell us something about how it is done and were rewarded by the following story:

WIRING THE WORLD'S TALLEST BUILDING
By William McCrom, Supt.,
L.K.Comstock and Company

Suppose you were to wire a whole town at one time, for lights, power, telephones. Not only that - suppose the town wasn't there when you started, but was being built up as you worked.

That will give you an idea of what it means to wire the tallest building man has yet put up. True, it was different from wiring a town in little details like installing 2-ton transformers on an 84th floor, one-quarter of a mile up in the air. Yet, the comparison is a fair one. The total transformer capacity of the Empire State Building is sufficient to light 156,000 fifty-watt lamps and the building telephone system, of the automatic type, has nearly 200 stations. There are many moderate sized towns whose electric requirements could easily be met by the installation in this one building.

How did we go about this big job ? First, by the most careful planning. That may sound trite, but it is a fact. Because of the large floor area of the tower stories, there had to be two riser shafts. (The Empire State is the first tall building in which this has been necessary). The size of the building, as a whole, required three transformer vaults, with high tension feeders to the transformers; five banks in the sub-basement, four banks on the 41st floor and another four banks on the 84th floor. And, the General Contractor required that, on reaching the 41st floor, the permanent banks of transformers be ready for temporary connections to hoisting engines and to lights.

So the details of all these had to be carefully planned before the work was started, along with data on panel drilling, cable supports and column and ceiling outlet boxes - both, in order that we could keep our own schedule and that we might tie our work in with that of the other trades. In this planning, we were greatly helped by the fact that the General Contractor had most efficiently organized the whole job, maintaining a definite sequence of operation week by week that resulted in a smooth running job and in each contractor being able to follow his schedule closely. Nevertheless, a building of this size presented many new problems to every trade. In tackling those that fell to us, we arrived at some solutions which could be applied to less imposing jobs with corresponding results of saving in time and work.

For example, in installing column boxes - we worked out a scheme of fastening strips of light-gauge perforated iron around the columns so that the boxes could be mounted on the strips and held out at the proper distance from the columns. Then, when the columns were walled up, the boxes would be in position and we would not have to break through to pull conduit. These strips or bands were made up on the job; one crew going ahead putting them up and attaching the outlet boxes with knockouts ready to receive the conduit, which was installed later by a follow-up crew - all this, of course, before the tiles were set.

PERMANENT ELECTRICAL INSTALLATION - Continued

For ceiling outlets, we used boxes four inches deep, with knockout near the top. The reason for this lies in an interesting departure from usual practice made by the engineers; namely, all steel girders and beams throughout the building are depressed below the level of the structural floor slab, bringing the top of the floor beams about two inches below the top of the slab. Thus, all distributing conduits from the panel boards were installed at one time, across the beams, without offsets, permitting them to be cast in the floor slab and resulting both in quicker installation of conduit and easier pulling of wire, because of the absence of bends.

Panel boxes, cable support boxes, T boxes and M boxes were all set one floor ahead of concrete on uprights of 2" angle iron. In this way, when crews arrived on the various floors to install conduit, everything was in place and ready for a speedy and a complete job, the conduit being terminated right into the panels without ripping out.

Throughout the building we used a color system on circuit wire and feeder cables; one color for each phase. This did away with testing for circuits and helped us push the job along. Cable was delivered in proper cutting lengths and tagged so that it could be put on the proper floor ahead of the pulling crew. For speedier lowering of the cable, we hung a 24" wheel from the ceiling and passed the cable over it into the conduit, with a power-driven winch on the other end to do the pulling. This worked so successfully that we found we could handle two sets of cables coming from two different conduits at the same time.

Another valuable departure from usual methods was worked out for laying the underfloor duct system, which was installed throughout the building for telephone and miscellaneous signal distribution. The duct was of the open-bottom type, and instead of laying the customary mats, we had the concrete men screed off the top of the floor slab along the route of the duct, before it had set, and trowel this surface. This made an excellent mat and after the first floor had set, the junction boxes and ducts were put in place along the areas that had been smoothed off. To hold the duct, we developed a wire clip that could be nailed to the concrete with a one-inch nail. Incidentally, our first order for these clips called for 80,000 - and that was only the first.

Now, as to those transformers on the 84th floor. Here was a problem - not only the transformers themselves, weighing about two tons each, but also the reels of high tension cable, each of which weighed about $2\frac{1}{2}$ tons. We solved it by building a railway! We ran the trucks transporting the transformers into the building, unloaded them by a traveling hoist onto flat cars and pushed the cars along narrow-gauge track onto a hod hoist. This took cars and transformers (or cable as the case might be) to the 78th floor where we passed them on by a relay hoist to the 84th floor. Here again, track was laid to the transformer room, the transformers run into the room and lifted by chain blocks to their permanent locations - a $2\frac{1}{2}$ hour journey from street to position.

PLUMBING

The plumbing installation was made by J.L.Murphy, Inc.,
340 East 44th St., N.Y.City

There is installed in the above building, 51 miles of plumbing piping.

There will be a reserve at all times of 90,000 gallons of water for domestic and fire purposes, although every fixture and every piece of piping may be supplied with water without the aid of any tanks.

Vitreous China plumbing fixtures have been installed to the number of 2500.

The fire-fighting system is the largest and most complete of its kind in any building. There is available for immediate use, eight miles of the best grade, linen fire hose.

The roof drainage system is separate and independent from the rest of the plumbing system. Rain water from certain sections of the building runs through a series of pipes for 1/2 a mile before it reaches the public sewer.

The sanitary drainage system carries water from certain plumbing fixtures a distance of 1300 ft. before it reaches the public sewer.

The water used for the upper section of the building is pumped from one open tank in the basement to a height of 1100 ft. - vertically, in one lift. This is the first time this has been accomplished in a building.

The Vacuum cleaning system is the largest of its type in the world. There are two separate systems; one from the lowest floor up to and including the 30th, and the other from the 31st floor to a distance of 1250 feet above the ground.

Due to the height of the building, the waste from the plumbing fixtures on the first floor and below runs to a separate system which discharges into an ejector from where it is forced to the public sewer.

There are six separate systems of hot and cold water.

The illuminating gas is carried through piping to a height of 1100 feet above the ground.

HEATING AND VENTILATING

The Heating and Ventilating work was installed by Baker, Smith & Co., Inc.
572-576 Greenwich Street, New York City.

About 54 miles of brass, steel and wrought iron pipe was used on the
heating, medium pressure and high pressure lines.

Approximately 2,300,000 lbs. of galvanized and black iron and copper
were used in connection with the ventilation work.

Radiators were installed to the number of 6,700 - containing a heating
surface of 247,000 square feet for the heating of the building.

These radiators will require approximately 90,000,000 to 100,000,000 lbs.
of steam per season for the direct heating of the building.

The supply and exhaust fans will handle approximately 1,150,000 cubic
feet of supply and exhaust air per minute.

It will require approximately 40,000,000 lbs. of steam per year to
temper the supply air.

LATHING AND PLASTERING

The following quantities have been submitted by Martin Conry & Sons,
Incorporated of 51 East 42nd St., N.Y.City. This firm did the
lathing and plastering work   *

10,000	Tons	of	Plaster (Neat and Finish
12,000	"	"	Sand
200	"	"	Wire Lath
300	"		Chanel and Furing Iron (Approx.1,000,000 l.ft.)
50	"	"	Corner Bead Material (Approximately 80 miles)

The total number of square feet of plastered surface area could be
expressed as a sidewalk area three feet in width, which would extend
for a distance of 360 miles, or from the Empire State Building to
the Capitol Building in Washington, D.C.

TILE AND TERRAZZO

The terrazzo and the floor and wall tile work was installed by the
DePaoli, Del Turco Foscato Corporation of New York City.

Terrazzo:

The area of terrazzo installed in the corridors is about 250,000
square feet. This area required the use of about 250,000 lineal
feet of brass strip for expansion joints. In weight, this brass
is equivalent to 90,000 lbs. or 45 tons of metal.

The materials used in the terrazzo were about 1,250 yds of sand,
about 12,500 bags of cement and 15,000 bags of marble chips.

The following kinds of marble chips were used :

       Botticino -   imported from Italy
       Belgian Black   "   "   Belgium
       Cardiff Green - from Maryland, U.S.A.

Tile:

The floor and wall tile work in toilets involved the following areas
and kinds of tile :-

    35,000 sq.ft. size 2-1/8" x 2-1/8" Black & White alternate floor
     8,500 " " 1-1/4" Hexagon white floor
   55,000 " " 6"x3" white glazed wall = 6875 tiles 440,000 ties
     3,000 lineal feet of 6" cove bottom round top black glazed base
     4,500 "   "   " 6" "   "   "   " white "   "

1115005 ties

INTERIOR MARBLE

All the interior marble work (except on the Main Floor) was done by the Traitel Marble Company.

The quantities involved, follow:

	Cardiff and Westfield Green Marble Base	Hauteville-Rocheron and St.Cecile Marble Panels and Wainscoting
Elevator Lobbies	16,834 sq.feet	84,539 sq.ft.
Corridor Core	17,395 " "	117,179 " "
Corridor Dotted Line	11,890 " "	80,259 " "
Total,	46,119 " "	281,977 " "

A Grand total of 328,096 square feet of this marble was used, weighing about 14 lbs. per square foot - bringing the total weight to approximately 2,297 tons.

The green Westfield Marble comes from Westfield, Mass.
The green Cardiff Marble comes from Cardiff, Md.
The Hauteville, Rocheron & St.Cecile Marbles are
imported from France

INTERIOR MARBLE - MAIN FLOOR

All of the interior marble furnished by William Bradley and Son, for the first floor of the building has been obtained from leading quarries of Europe.

The walls of all entrance halls, corridors and elevator lobbies, have a base course of Belgian Black from Belgium. Above this base, all the pilasters, door trim and panels throughout are finished in Est Rellante and Formosa Rose Marble from Germany. These marbles are also used on the stairways leading from the first to the second floor and, also, for the stairways from the first floor to the basement, with treads of Travertine marble from Italy.

The floors of all entrances, lobbies and corridors throughout, are furnished in blue Belge marble from Belgium for the borders, with the field of Red Levanto marble from Italy and Bois Jordan marble from France.

Summed up, the marbles used on the first floor consist of two colors from Germany; two from Belgium ; two from Italy and one from France.

Great difficulty was experienced in securing this beautiful harmony in colors, selected by the Architects. A special representative was sent to Europe to report conditions and insure the possibility of these marbles being received in time. It was also necessary to place a representative at the quarries to prevent delays in shipments.

There is no doubt that this is one of the very best jobs in the United States in tone and harmony of colors.

A special feature of the marble work is the ornamental panel facing the visitor who enters the Fifth Avenue doorway. Between strips of bronze there are marble inserts representing maps of New York and adjacent territory with a gauge which registers the direction in which the wind is blowing at the top of the building, 1,252 feet above the floor upon which the visitor stands.

Some idea may be gained of the immense amount of work required on the marble inserts for the panel by the fact that it was necessary to make eighty different patterns for the marble to be cut to size. As an illustration, these marble pieces show every bay in the shore line of Long Island and only expert carvers could be employed in cutting it. The ornamental strips of metal had to be sunk in the marble and difficult channels for same were cut to the most accurate lines. In addition to these difficulties, the marble had to be selected in order to secure the necessary harmonious blend of colors to bring out the artistic design of the Architects.

ROOFING

Tuttle Roofing Company of 522 East 20th Street, New York City, have
used the following material quantities in connection with their
roofing contract :

Roofing Work: 1,100 rolls, single-ply (400 sq.ft.to roll) Tar Paper

               500 Barrels, Pitch
     77,200 Sq. ft. 1" Cork Insulation
   185,500 Pieces 6" x 9" x 1" Roofing Tile
     1,600 Bags Cement
       260 Yards Sand

Side-walk Arches and Tank Room Floors:

       400 Rolls Tar Paper
       200 Barrels Pitch

Finished Cement Floor - Temporary Protection:

   20,000 rolls heavy Tomahawk Paper (1 Square Each)
      100 drums asphalt
    1,000 Gallons Fuel Oil

METAL WINDOWS

The double-hung metal window units, which were used throughout the
85 stories, except on the first and second floors, numbered 6,305
windows.

     600 Tons of Steel were used in the manufacture of these
         windows

     130,000 feet of Sash Chain

     450 Tons of Sash Weights

     12,000 lbs. of bronze was used in manufacturing the
         hardware for these windows.

We are further advised by the Campbell Metal Window Corporation of
New York, who furnished and installed the windows, that it
required ninety cars to transport the windows from their plant in
Baltimore to New York.

LUPTON SASH

Casement windows were furnished and installed on second floor by
David Lupton Sons Company of Philadelphia.

MAIL CHUTES

In planning the Empire State Building, the Architects fully appreciated the necessity of providing adequate and dependable Mail Service for tenants. The equipment, designed to meet the needs of the twenty thousand tenants who will occupy the building, and the technical problem presented by its unpresented height of eighty-six stories, consists of eight Cutler Mail Chutes of the Model "F" type, of the latest and most approved form, the outcome of fifty years' experience of the makers in meeting the exacting demands of public use under Post Office Regulation.

These chutes are arranged in pairs, and by means of a device which can be operated only by Post Office Officials, the chutes are closed on alternate floors dividing the mail and reducing the risk of congestion by overcrowding. In case one of the chutes in any pair is in need of cleaning, or repair, it can be closed throughout its entire length, and the mail service continued temporarily by means of the other.

The mail boxes are of aluminum and bronze, richly ornamented, from the special design of the Architects.

While the amount of material used in this installation is trifling, as compared with the great quantity of steel, stone, etc. of which this vast structure is built, the installation is the largest of its kind with 396 openings for the deposit of mail and, if placed in a single line would measure approximately a mile.

The Mail Chute, like the elevator, is one of the modern devices that makes the upper stories of a building, no matter how far above ground, as valuable for rental purposes as those below.

The installation was made by Cutler Mail Chute Company, whose general offices are at Rochester, New York.

HOLLOW METAL DOORS AND TRIM

The hollow metal doors and base moulding were furnished by the J.C.McFarland Company, Inc., associated with the Metal Door & Trim Company, Inc., of New York City.

The advise us that the items furnished and installed are as follows:

According to Plans

   1,900 Door Openings
122,000 ft. of Base, including that for Radiator Fronts

Attic Stock

1,200 Door Openings
25,000 ft. Base Moulding

DAMPPROOFING

All of the common brick backing up the exterior limestone and metal
trim was covered with a plastic waterproofing compound before plaster
was applied. The only exception made to this procedure was in the
radiator recesses where a waterproof paint was used instead of the
compound.

This waterproofing was applied by the Hydro-Bar Corporation of New
York City and we have been informed by them that 1,096 barrels of
Trowel Mastic were used and the area covered is 660,000 sq. ft.

This work was begun July 14th, 1930 and save for a few odds and ends,
was completed on December 10,1930.

EXTERIOR CALKING

The work of calking around metal window frames and cast aluminum
spandrels and between the chrome nickel steel trim and stonework
on the exterior of the building, was done by Ev-Air-Tight Calking
Company of Philadelphia.

This Company used 35 tons of Pecora Calking Compound to complete
their contract.

HOW THE SUPERINTENDENT CAN PUT SAFETY ON THE JOB

A careful Superintendent appreciates, first of all, that he is not only the custodian of the property of his employers, but in a higher moral sense, he is also the protector of the lives of those working under him and of the public coming in contact with his building operation.

Starting with the inherent respect for the sanctity of human life, it follows, naturally that he will encourage every agency seeking to put safety on the job.

The indifferent Superintendent is the one who makes safety inspectors understand by his actions - and often by his words, that they are so many busybodies concerned only with the interfering with the speedy progress of the work and adding needless expense to his job.

This type of Superintendent who will not offer a reasonable measure of safety cooperation, is not only jeopardizing the lives of his employes but he is misrepresenting the attitude of responsible building employers. The proof of that statement is demonstrated by our presence here tonight at this session of the Safety Conference which is sponsored by the Building Trades Employers Association.

SAFETY METHODS EMPLOYED ON EMPIRE STATE BUILDING

Let us review briefly some of the efforts taken by the Superintendent to put safety on the Empire State Building job :-

Safety Personnel:
First, he appointed an assistant to supervise and coordinate all safety agencies on the building. This Assistant Superintendent was the contact man to whom the State Labor Inspection, City Inspector, Insurance and Subcontractors' safety men could go with complaints and suggestions. They could go to him with the complete assurance that they would be received courteously and the complaints given immediate attention.

The Assistant Superintendent placed two carpenter foremen directly in charge of building the temporary protection work. At one stage of the work at least 50 men were employed in these two gangs. These men, together with the other foremen on the job were given to understand that they constituted a permanent safety committee and members of the protection gangs were told to correct immediately any dangerous condition brought to their attention in order to save time and avoid **accidents.**

The State Labor Department Inspector always made a list of his recommendations in triplicate form. One copy he gave to the carpenter protection foreman in the field; one copy to the Asst.Supt., and the third copy was retained by himself. After a reasonable length of time he returned to the job and checked back over each recommendation to see if his instructions had been carried out.

It so happened, that the Insurance Company carrying the liability insurance for the General Contractor, also carried insurance for the Elevator Contractor.

Safety Personnel (Continued):

This insurance company's safety engineer exercised the strictest
supervision over the matter of making the elevator contractor refrain
from breaking down barricades around the shafts and made certain the
General Contractor provided adequate safety planking in all shafts
to prevent materials dropping on the elevator men thereby avoiding
third-party accident cases from both companies.

DEMOLITION WORK

At the start of demolition work on the Waldorf Astoria Hotel Buildings
which was done by the General Contractor, the permanent sidewalk bridge
was erected with office buildings on the Fifth Avenue section.

This bridge covered every legal requirement, but we were convinced that
a building operation of such a character demands a bridge extending
from building line to building line if the public is to be accorded
an adequate measure of protection.

All of the structural steel was burned with oxy-acetylene torches and
lowered to the streets for loading on trucks, but as much as possible
of the loading was done in Astor Court, a private street extending
through the property.

A scaffold extending 12 feet from the face of the building with a 3-ft.
baffle, was erected and reconstructed during the downward course of
the demolition work. In reality, two complete scaffolds were used,
the lower one being in place, while the upper one was being removed.
All windows were boarded in stories directly below where floor arches
were being broken down. One complete story was wrecked at a time and
all debris was dumped into wooden chutes located within the building,
extending from the floor upon which the wrecking was being done down
through to the Main Floor.

Practically all loading of debris was done inside the building - away
from the general public.

Strict care was taken to employ skilled wreckers only and other trades
were kept as much as possible, outside the wrecking zones. Skilled
wreckers have worked out a system of signs and symbols which indicate
to them danger spots. A small piece of lath or trim nailed across a
door, indicates to all other wreckers that this entrance is not to be
used. A crude circle of sticks on a floor marks a zone over which a
floor is about to be broken down. To the unitiated these signs mean
nothing - and the ignoring of them might result in death.

No fatalties occurred during the demolition of the superstructure of
the hotel buildings and this was one of the most difficult wrecking
jobs ever attempted. Nearly 25,000 loads of material constituted the
wreckage.

ERECTION OF EMPIRE STATE BUILDING

All job offices for subcontractors were placed on Second Floor and
built of corrugated metal exterior to lessen fire hazard.

The Main Floor was kept free of buildings in order to allow ample
room for delivery of materials. At the busiest period nearly 500
trucks per day were unloaded.

Erection of Empire State Building (Continued):

At one stage of its development, three apron scaffolds at different floor levels extended completely around all sides of the building.

Rope nets were used to enclose stories where floor arch forms were being stripped and tarpaulins were used on floors to enclose floors below where concrete was being poured, to prevent drip from being blown into streets.

A close watch was kept on pipe scaffold around mooring mast tower to prevent icicles from forming and falling into the street. This pipe scaffold constructed by Chesbro-Whitman Co. with firesafe planks and wire enclosures, is the last word in safety construction.

Special 200 H.P. hoist engines were built with special steel cages and car platforms capable of raising four tons. All engines were equipped with special automatic motor brakes mounted on motor shafts and dial indicators to show engineer the floor landing, thereby eliminating the necessity of watching cable markings. All cars had landing dogs or lugs on underside of car platform.

An ingenious automatic electrical signal system devised by an electrician on the job eliminated the use of bell ropes for signaling system.

The use of an industrial railway system and overhead trolley unloading system, in conjunction with these material hoists, permitted practically all of the material (except structural steel) to be raised inside the building, thereby removing a serious hazard to the general public. Fortunately, not a piece of steel was dropped during the hoisting of 58,000 tons of structural steel.

All regular bellmen assigned to the hoists were kept on duty while hoists were being used by subcontractors.

All temporary hoist shaftways were enclosed with heavy wire screen panels for full floor heights.

These safety features and many others are fully described in Safety Bulletin No.10 of Building Trades Employers Association.

Every effort was made to discourage foremen from favoring certain men for overtime work on hazardous jobs - such as raising shaft heads - where the element of fatigue plays such a dangerous part.

Special attention was paid to prevent the throwing of rivets towards the outside of the building where a miss might mean a death in the street below and to eliminate danger to workmen on the building, it was tried to place forges as near as possible to the riveting gangs.

In conclusion, it can be said that no expense was spared and an honest effort was made to put safety on the job - yet, it remains a sad fact that six workmen and one pedestrian lost their lives not through indifference on the part of those in charge, but rather, due to the normal hazards of modern building construction.

SAFETY AND PROTECTION WORK

A malicious propaganda in the form of rumors and subtle press articles, became widespread during the construction period. The impression created was that adequate protection of human life was entirely disregarded in the feverish anxiety of all concerned in the project to establish a record for speed in the construction of the building.

These press articles which appeared in various sections of the country, were undoubtedly inspired by political animosity, inasmuch as they charged by innuendo that a nationally prominent politician who was at the head of the enterprise, was responsible for having the public agencies suppress all information regarding the number of workmen killed on the building. At one time these rumors persisted in having the number killed as high as 64 men - or, one life for every story of the building erected up to that time.

These character assassins, who became so expert in villification during the Presidential campaign of 1928, would try to make a gullible public believe (especially in the hinterland) that a man like former Governor, Alfred E.Smith would sponsor such a condition and then suppress the true facts from becoming known.

They seem to forget that all who have known him since his earliest days as a legislator respect him as a consistent champion of human rights. Even the most ardent of his political opponents in this State will be forced to admit that he has been responsible for the enactment of more benificent social legislation than any other single individual. He will live in history, not only as a great statemen but, better still, as a great humanitarian.

There is no doubt that more money was spent on this building (in proportion to its size) for temporary protection work and safety appliances than was ever spent on any building operation of like character before.

Three agencies, The City of New York Building Department, The New York State Labor Department and the Employers Liability Assurance Corporation had their safety engineers and inspectors constantly in attendance to see that the safety measures provided were adequate and in compliance with the ordinances of the City of New York and the rules of the State Department of Labor.

In addition, Post & McCord, Otis Elevator Company and other subcontractors had their own safety inspectors constantly on the job.

A committee was appointed by the Building Trades Employers Association to investigate the rumors mentioned and were so favorably impressed with the safety features employed, that they incorporated their findings in a special safety bulletin to be distributed generally, among builders.

Seven people lost their lives as the result of accidents from the start of the wrecking of the Waldorf-Astoria buildings(one of the most difficult demolition jobs ever attempted) until the completion of the Empire State Building.

It is an extremely regrettable fact that this happened, but these lives were lost through accidents which occurred due to the normal hazards of modern buildings and certainly not, as charged, to inhuman indifference and neglect.

Gov. Smith speaking at the cornerstone
laying ceremony.

*On September 9, 1930, just twelve months after the first
building contracts were signed, former Governor Alfred E.
Smith, president of the Empire State Corporation, addressed
the crowd at the traditional cornerstone laying ceremony.
The steel work topped out ten days later. (#274 9/9/30)*

Mooring Mast finished and topped off.
Flag - 1266 feet above sidewalk.

*Just six months after the September 30th topping off of the
steel frame of the eighty-six floor office tower, workers raised
the flag over the completed mooring mast. (#543 5:42PM
3/18/31)*

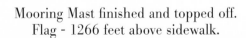

Safety and Protection Work - Continued:

Unsung Heroes of Peace:

Every large construction project exacts its toll of human life.
Accidents and fatalities occur which are all a part of the story but,
generally, constitute a chapter which remains unrecorded.

Each skyscraper, bridge, dam, acqueduct, tunnel and subway claims
its victims who make the supreme sacrifice in the performance of their
daily tasks.

Grateful peoples, the World over, honor their dead by placing commem-
orative plaques of bronze upon monuments, office buildings and factories.
We read the names of the men who fell, each inscribed opposite a gold
star to indicate that their friends appreciate their sacrifices and
honor their memory.

Let us show similar reverence and respect for our fellow-workmen who
have sacrificed their lives in the pursuits of peace.

These six men lost their lives while working on the Empire State Building:

January 31,1930	Giuseppi Tedeschi	Laborer
January 31,1930	L. DeDominichi	Laborer
April 29,1930	Reuben Brown	Ironworker
July 14,1930	Sigus Andreasen	Carpenter
July 30,1930	Frank Sullivan	Carpenter
December 9,1930	A.Carlson	Carpenter

On July 11, 1930, Miss Elizabeth Eagher, while crossing 34th Street,
west of Fifth Avenue, was struck on the ankle by a piece of broken
ironworker's plank. She sustained a fractured ankle and it was
reported to us that blood poisoning resulted in her death.

They are numbered among the unsung heroes of peace.

It would be a thoughtful act to inscribe their names upon the bronze
plaque which will bear the names of those other workmen who were the
recipients of the craftsmanship award certificates.

A sentimental gesture, think you ? Well, perhaps - but, also, an
acknowledgement of our debt to them, as well as our universal kinship
with Him, who was also once a humble toiler in the guise of the lowly
Carpenter of Nazareth.

Mooring Mast finished and partly stripped
of scaffolding.

*This view shows the final form of the building free of all
temporary construction structures other than scaffolding
on the lower half of the mooring mast. The mast is finished, and the scaffolding is being removed from the top
down. (#544 3/21/31)*

CONCLUSION

A quotation from Ruskin, which has been used frequently as an
inspirational thought in connection with building, follows:

> "Therefore, when we build, let us think that we build forever.
> Let it not be for present delight, nor for present use alone,
> let it be such work as our decendants will thank us for, and
> let us think, as we lay stone on stone, that a time is to
> come when these stones will be held sacred, because our hands
> have touched them, and that men will say as they look upon
> the labor and the wrought substance of them - "See, ! this,
> our fathers did for us ."

The Empire State Building is constructed to stand the rigors of
future centuries. What its span of life will be in this
ever-changing world - no man can foretell. Perhaps it will live
on to see old Empires crumble and new dynasties arise, mellowing
with the passage of time, down through the future ages.

Or, perhaps, the rapidly changing economic conditions of a new
era will precipitate its destruction sooner than we care to
anticipate. Conditions which in our own time, dictated the doom
of its aristocratic predecessor, the old Waldorf-Astoria Hotel,
together with the architectural gem that was the near neighbor
of the old hotel - Madison Square Garden.

At the moment, however, we are astounded at the marvel of its birth.
Title to the old hotel was acquired by the Owners on June 1, 1929.
Demolition of the old buildings was started on September 22, 1929
and completely finished on March 12, 1930. The first steel columns
for the new Empire State Building were set on April 7,1930 and the
building was completely finished on March 1, 1931. Within a period
of twenty-one months, the entire project was conceived and brought
to successful execution.

This massive building now stands as a majestic symbol of the enterprise
and efficiency of our age - offering mute tribute to promoter, financier,
architect, engineer, builder, artisan and everyone who toiled to make
it a reality - down to the humblest laborer.

Viewed in the light of Faith, it stands out clearly against the
sky as a noble monument reflecting the glory of God, Who had given
such power to man.

ANALYSIS OF COST

GC14 Plant and Equipment

Subdivision	Labor	Material	Proportion GC10 Power Work	Ins.on all Labor	Total	Items To Be Pro-Rated
Foundations	403.34	51,252.11	5,000.00	24.20	56,679.65	
Stone	14,150.00	18,562.58	--	1,217.77	33,930.35	
Guy Derricks	1,546.36	2,934.98	1,000.00	92.78	5,574.12	
Hoists	95,595.65	105,617.02	17,000.00	5,735.74	223,948.41	Pro-R 23% Mas;15% Arches;8% Stone;54% to balance Pro-R on basis of Time of Engineers
Indus.Rwy.	13,924.78	9,626.64	--	835.49	24,386.91	50% misc 8% stone; 42% Mas.
Overhead Trol.	1,267.54	3,503.01	500.00	76.05	5,346.60	25% to misc;75% to stone
Concrete Equip.	2,207.76	7,683.52	500.00	132.47	10,523.75	25% to found;25% misc; 50% arches
Mixing Plants	5,237.00	7,358.10	1,500.00	314.22	14,409.32	50% arch 5% stone; 25% Mas; 20% misc.
(2) Mine Cages & Instal.opengs.	36,733.61	21,597.58	2,000.00	2,204.02	62,535.21	
(4) A.B.See Open. & Mtce.	19,111.64	4,065.68	--	1,146.70	24,324.02	
A.B.See Instal. By Otis	50,600.00	--	--	--	50,600.00	
Temp.Open.& Mat. of Otis Cars	13,244.97	1,800.00	--	794.70	15,839.67	
Granite	421.09	87.82	--	25.26	534.17	
Tower Hoist	1,464.43	--	400.00	87.86	1,952.29	

GC2 Superv'sn Payroll $230,000.00 Net Labor Distributed To

Subs.	60,000.00
Masonry	$51,000.00
Arches	23,800.00
Stone	20,400.00
Rough Carp.	3,400.00
Foundations	27,200.00
Gen.Cond.	44,200.00
	$230,000.00

EMPIRE STATE BUILDING

Cost of Face Bricks - Laid in Place

Account	Labor		Amount

M-3   Labor   For Bricklayers Apprentices, Bricklayers, Laborers, Hoisting Engineers, etc. $48,548.06

       Insurance   Average rate 8.516   4,134.35

GC14   Hod Hoist   Labor   Proportion Hod Hoist, Plant & Equip.   1,319.21

                  Insurance   6%   79.15

GC14   Industrial Railway   Labor   Proportion Industrial Rwy.   351.50

                  Insurance   6%   21.09

GC14   Mixing Plants   Labor   Proportion Mortar Mixing Plants,   78.55

                  Insurance   6%   4.71

GC2   General Supervision   Labor   Proportion General Organization Payroll   3,060.00

                  Insurance   Rate 1.75   53.55

MT   Maintenance   Labor   Proportion Maintenance Equipment   174.60

                  Insurance   8.516   14.86

     Cost of Laying 835,757 Face Bricks   57,839.63
     Gross Labor Cost per 1000 Face Bricks $69.21

Material

M-3	Material - Face Bricks, Lime, Sand, Cement, Etc.	34,409.21
GC14	" Proportion Hod Hoist, Plant and Equipment	1,759.30
GC14	" Proportion Industrial Railway	230.59
GC14	" Proportion Mixing Plants	132.87
MT	Proportion Maintenance, Power, oil, gas, water, etc.	175.57

     Material Cost laying 835,757 face bricks   36,707.54
     Gross material cost laying 1000 face bricks, $43.91

     Gross Labor and Material Cost Laying 1000 Face bricks, $113.12

Net Labor Units	No. Laid	Acct.	Straight Time	Excess Time	Total
Face Bricks Laid in Place	835,757	M-3	55.42	1.69	57.11

Ratio Bricklayers	Laborers	Production Per 8-Hr. Day Bricklayers
1	.9	624

EMPIRE STATE BUILDING

Cost of Common Brick Laid in Place
Back of Limestone and Interior Walls

Account	Labor	Amount
M2,M5,M4	Labor, Bricklayers Apprentices Bricklayers, Laborers,Hoisting Eng.etc.	$353,620.52
	Insurance - average rate 8.516%	30,114.32
GC14 Hod Hoist -	Labor, proportion Hod Hoist, Plant & Equip.	10,333.88
	Insurance, 6%	620.03
GC14 Indus.Rwy. -	Labor proportion Industrial Rwy.	2,753.44
	Insurance, 6%	165.20
GC14 Mixing Plants-	Labor, proportion Mortar Mix.Plants	615.34
	Insurance, 6%	36.91
GC2	Labor - proportion Gen. Organiz.Payroll	23,970.00
	Insurance 1.75%	419.47
MT	Labor - proportion Maintenance or Equip.	1,367.59
	Insurance, 8.516%	116.46
	Labor Cost laying 10,258,628 Com.Bricks	424,133.17

Gross Labor Cost per 1000 bricks,$41.34

Material

M2,M5,M4	Common Brick, Lime,Sand,Cement, Plant,etc.	254,905.43
GC14	Material, proportion Hod Hoist plant & Equip.	13,322.07
GC14	Material, proportion Industrial Railway	1,806.30
GC14	Material, proportion Mixing Plants	1,040.81
MT	Proportion Mainten.power,oil,gas,water,etc.	1,375.33
	Material Cost Laying 10,258,628 Com.Bricks	272,449.94

Gross Material Cost laying 1000 Br. $26.56

Gross Labor and Material Cost
laying 1000 common bricks, $67.90

Net Labor Units

	No.Laid		Straight Time	Excess Time	Total
Common Brick,Backing Limestone	8,877,700	M2	32.22	1.97	34.19
Interior Common Brick	1,227,467	M5	36.51	.82	37.33
Common Brick at Lot Line Wall	153,461	M4	27.44	.21	27.65

	Ratio Bricklayers	Laborers	Proportion per 8-hr.Bricklayers
Common Brick,Backing Limest.	1	1.1	864
Interior Common Brick	1	1.4	858
Common Brick at Lot Line Wall	1	1.2	1052

EMPIRE STATE BUILDING

Cost of 2" Smooth and Scored, Solid Column
Covering Laid in Place

Account	Labor	
P6 and P7	Labor - for Bricklayers, apprentices, bricklayers' laborers, hoisting engineers, etc.	$84,873.43
	Insurance - average rate 8.516	7,227.82
GC14	Labor - Proportion Hod Hoist, Plant & Equipment	2,198.69
	Insurance, 6%	131.92
GC14	Labor - Proportion Industrial Railway	585.83
	Insurance, 6%	35.15
GC14	Labor - Proportion Mortar Mixing Plants	130.92
	Insurance, 6%	7.85
GC2	Labor - Proportion General Organization Payroll	5,100.00
	Insurance, 1.75%	89.25
MT	Labor - Proportion Maintenance of Equipment	290.00
	Insurance 8.516%	24.70

Gross Labor Cost Laying (33,845 pcs.2x12x12 scor-ed) $100,695.56
(342,098 " 2¼ x8 x 12 ")
(11,740 " 2x12x12 smooth)
(140,272" 2¼x8x12 smooth)

Gross Labor Cost per   367,164 square feet
Square foot $.277

Material

Account		Material	
P6 & P7	Material - Tile, lime, sand, cement, etc.		50,863.96
GC14	" Proportion Hod Hoist, Plant and Equipment		2,820.19
GC14	" " Industrial Railway		384.31
GC14	" " Mixing Plants		221.44
MT	" " Maintenance, power,water,gas,oil,etc.		293.00

Gross Material Cost $54,582.90
Square Foot, Material Cost $.148

Gross Labor and Material Cost, per square foot, $.425

Net Labor Units

Sq.Feet Laid	Account	Straight Time	Excess Time	Total	Ratio Bricklayers	Lab.	Production per 8-Hr. Day, Bricklaye
367,164	P6 and P7	.223	.008	.231	1	1.3	194

EMPIRE STATE BUILDING

Cost of 3"x12"x12" Scored and Smooth Partition Tile Laid in Place

LABOR

Account

P-3 - Labor for Bricklayers-Apprentices-Bricklayers Laborers) $25,060.11
Hoisting Engineers, etc. (
Insurance - Average Rate - 8.516 - - - - - - - - - - - - - - 2,134.12
GC14- Labor - Proportion Hod Hoist Plant & Equipt- - - - - 659.61
Insurance - 6% - 39.58
GC14- Labor - Proportion Industrial Railway Plant & Equipt - 175.75
Insurance - 6% - 10.54
GC14- Labor - Proportion Mortar Mixing Plants- - - - - - - 39.27
Insurance - 6% - 2.36

GC2 - Labor - Proportion General Organization Payroll- - - - 1,530.00
Insurance - 1.75 - 26.77

MT - Labor - Proportion Maintenance of Equipt - - - - - - - 87.78
Insurance - 8.516- 7.47

141,229 Pcs - Gross Labor Cost Laying 6"x12"x12" Scored and) $29,773.36
Smooth Partition Tile (
Gross Labor Cost Laying 1 Square Ft $.211

MATERIAL

P-3 - Material - 3"x12"x12" Tile-Lime-Sand-Cement, etc. - - $11,795.81
GC14- Material - Proportion Hod Hoist Plant & Equipt - - - - 846.06
GC14- Material - Proportion Industrial Railway - - - - - - - 115.29
GC14- Material - Proportion Mixing Plants- - - - - - - - - - 66.43
MT - Material - Proportion Maintenance-Power-Oil-Gas-Water,
etc.- 87.78

Gross Material Cost Laying 141,229 Pcs. 3"x12"x12" Tile $12,911.37
Gross Material Cost Per Square Foot $.091

Gross Labor and Material Cost 1 Sq.Ft. 3" Tile - $.302

NET LABOR UNITS

No. Pieces Laid	Account	Straight Time	Excess Time	Total	Ratio Bricklayers	Laborers	Production Per 8 Hr.Day Bricklayer
141,229 pcs.	P-3	.17	.007	.177	1	1.2	166

EMPIRE STATE BUILDING

Cost of 4"x12"x12" Scored Partition Tile Laid in Place

LABOR

Account

P-4 - Labor for Bricklayers-Apprentices-Bricklayers Laborers) $60,233.93
 Hoisting Engineers, etc (

 Insurance - Average Rate - 8.516 - - - - - - - - - - - - 5,129.52
GC14- Labor - Proportion Hod Hoist Plant & Equipt- - - - - - - 1,539.08
 Insurance - 6% - 92.34
GC14- Labor - Proportion Industrial Railway Plant & Equipt - - 410.08
 Insurance - 6% - 24.60
GC14- Labor - Proportion Mortar Mixing Plants- - - - - - - - - 91.65
 Insurance - 6% - 5.50

GC2 - Labor - Proportion General Organization Payroll- - - - - 3,570.00
 Insurance - 1.75%- 62.47

MT - Labor - Proportion Maintenance of Equipt - - - - - - - - 204.83
 Insurance - 8.516- 17.44

304,139 Pcs. - 4"x12"x12" - Gross Labor Cost - - - - - - - - -$71,381.44

Gross Labor Cost Per Square Foot $.234

MATERIAL

P-4 - Material - Tile-Lime-Sand-Cement, etc. - - - - - - - - - -$27,640.49
GC14- Material - Proportion Hod Hoist Plant and Equipment- - - - 1,947.13
GC14- Material - Proportion Industrial Railway - - - - - - - - 269.02
GC14- Material - Proportion Mixing Plants - - - - - - - - - -- 155.01
MT - Material - Proportion Maintenance-Power-Water-Gas-Oil,etc 204.82

 Gross Material Cost - - - - - - - - - - - - - - -$30,216.47

Square Foot Gross Material Cost $.099

Gross Labor and Material Cost Per Sq. Ft. - $.333

NET LABOR UNITS

No. Pieces Laid	Account	Straight Time	Excess Time	Total	Ratio Bricklayers	Laborers	Production Per 8 Hour Day Bricklayer
304,139	P-4	.19	.008	.198	1	1.4	170

EMPIRE STATE BUILDING

Cost of 6"x12"x12" Scored Partition Tile Laid in Place

LABOR

Account

P-5 - Labor for Bricklayers-Apprentices-Bricklayers Laborers) $65,802.26
            Hoisting Engineers, etc. (
       Insurance - Average Rate - 8.516 - - - - - - - - - - - - - 5,603.82
GC14- Labor - Proportion Hod Hoist Plant and Equipt- - - - - 1,758.96
       Insurance - 6% - 105.54
GC14- Labor - Proportion Industrial Railway- - - - - - - - - 468.67
       Insurance - 6% - 28.12
GC14- Labor - Proportion Mortar Mixing Plants- - - - - - - - 104.74
       Insurance - 6% - 6.28

GC2 - Labor - Proportion General Organization Payroll- - - - - 4,080.00
       Insurance - 1.75%- 71.40

MT - Labor - Proportion Maintenance of Equipment- - - - - - 232.78
       Insurance - 8.516% - - - - - - - - - - - - - - - - - - - 19.82

Gross Labor Cost Laying 307,458 Pieces 6" Scored Partition Tile $78,282.39
Gross Labor Cost Per Square Foot $.2546

MATERIAL

P-5 - Material - Tile-Lime-Sand-Cement-etc. - - - - - - - - - -$37,289.14
GC14- Material - Proportion Hod Hoist Plant & Equipt- - - - - 2,256.15
GC14- Material - Proportion Industrial Railway- - - - - - - - 307.45
GC14- Material - Proportion Mixing Plants - - - - - - - - - - 177.16
PT - Material - Proportion Maintenance-Power-Water-Gas-Oil-etc 234.09

           Gross Material Cost - - - - - - - -$40,263.99
      Square Foot Material cost $.131

Gross Labor and Material Cost Per Sq.Ft. $.3856

NET LABOR UNITS

No. Pieces Laid	Account	Straight Time	Excess Time	Total	Bricklayers	Ratio Laborers	Production Per 8 Hour Day Bricklayer
307,458 Pcs.	P-5	.20	.014	.214	1	1.6	170

EMPIRE STATE BUILDING

Cost of 8" Scored Partition Tile - Laid in Place

LABOR

Account

P-8 - Labor for Bricklayers-Apprentices-Bricklayers Laborers) $3,068.31
              Hoisting Engineers, etc.   (
        Insurance - Average Rate 8.516 - - - - - - - - - - - - -   261.13
GC14- Labor - Proportion Hod Hoist Plant and Equipt- - - - - -   200.00
        Insurance - 6% -   12.00
GC14- Labor - Proportion Mortar Mixing Plants- - - - - - - - -   25.00
        Insurance - 6% -   1.50
GC2 - Labor - Proportion General Organization Payroll- - - - -   500.00
        Insurance - 1.75%- - - - - - - - - - - - - - - - - - -   8.75
MT - Labor- Proportion Maintenance of Equipt- - - - - - - - -   30.00
        Insurance - 8.516% - - - - - - - - - - - - - - - - - -   2.40
GC14- Labor - Proportion Industrial Railway- - - - - - - - - -   50.00
        Insurance - 6% -   3.00

Gross Labor Cost Laying 10,595 Pcs. 8"x12"x12" Partition Tile - $4,162.09

Gross Labor Cost Per Square Foot $.393

MATERIAL

P-8 - Material - Tile-Lime-Sand-Cement-etc. - - - - - - - - - - $2,164.83
GC14-   "   - Proportion Hod Hoist Plant & Equipt- - - - -   250.00
GC14-   "   - Proportion Industrial Railway- - - - - - - -   30.00
GC14-   "   - Proportion Mixing Plants - - - - - - - - - -   20.00
MT -   "   - Proportion Maintenance-Power-Water-Gas-Oil-&c   28.00

                        Gross Material Cost - - - - - $2,492.83

          Square Foot Gross Material Cost $.235

      Gross Labor and Material Cost Per Square Foot $.628

NET LABOR UNITS

No. Pieces Laid	Account	Straight Time	Excess Time	Total	Bricklayers	Ratio Laborers	Production Per 8 Hour Day Bricklayer
10,595	P-8	.285	.005	.29	1	1.9	150

EMPIRE STATE BUILDING

Cost of 6" Smooth Partition Tile Laid in Place

LABOR

Account

P-2 - Labor for Bricklayers-Apprentices-Bricklayers Laborers) Hoisting Engineers, etc. (	$140,284.48
Insurance - Average Rate 8.516 - - - - - - - - - - - - -	11,947.63
GC14- Hod Hoist- Labor-Proportion Hod Hoist Plant & Equipt - -	3,516.81
Insurance - 6% - - - - - - - - - - - - - - -	191.00
GC14- Industrial Railway- Labor-Proportion Industrial Railway & Equipt-	937.34
Insurance - 6% - - - - - - - - - - - - - -	56.24
GC14- Mixing Plants - Labor-Proportion Mortar Mixing Plants - - - -	209.48
Insurance - 6% - - - - - - - - - - - - - -	12.57
GC2 - General Supn - Labor-Proportion General Organization Payroll	8,160.00
Insurance - 1.75- - - - - - - - - - - - - -	142.80
MT - Maintenance-Labor - Proportion Maintenance Equipt- - - -	465.40
Insurance - 8.516- - - - - - - - - - - - -	39.63

Gross Cost of Laying 6"x12"x12" Smooth Partition Tile-632,413 $165,963.38
                                                      Pcs.

Gross Cost Laying 1 Sq.Ft. - 6x12x12 Smooth Partition Tile $.2624

MATERIAL

P-2 - Material - 6"x12"x12" Tile-Lime-Sand-Cement, etc.- - - -	$115,267.27
GC14- Material - Proportion Hod Hoist Plant & Equipt- - - - --	4,512.31
GC14- Material - Proportion Industrial Railway - - - - - - - -	614.91
GC14- Material - Proportion Mixing Plants - - - - - - - - --	354.32
MT - Material - Proportion Maintenance-Power-Oil-Gas-Water,etc	468.20

Material Cost Laying 632,413 Pcs. - 6"x12"x12" Smooth
                                          Partition Tile - - - -- $121,217.01

Gross Material Cost per Square Foot $.1916

Gross Labor and Material Cost 1 Sq. Ft. 6" Smooth Tile - $.4540

NET LABOR UNITS

6"x12"x12" Smooth Partition Tile Laid in Place

No. Pieces Laid	Account	Straight Time	Excess Time	Total	Ratio Bricklayer	Laborer	Production Per 8 Hour Day Bricklayer
632,413	P-2	$.21	$.01	$.22	1	1.5	154

Cost of Patching all Brick and Tile Masonry Work

Labor

Account

P-14 - Labor for Bricklayers-Apprentices-Bricklayers Laborers) $67,738.46
              Hoisting Engineers, etc.   (
       Insurance - Rate 8.516% - - - - - - - - - - - - - - - - -   5,768.60
GC14 - Labor - Proportion Hod Hoist Plant & Equipt - - - - -   659.60
       Insurance - 6% - - - - - - - - - - - - - - - - - - --   39.57
GC14 - Labor - Proportion Industrial Railway Plant & Equipt- -   175.75
       Insurance - 6% - - - - - - - - - - - - - - - - - - --   10.54
GC14 - Labor - Proportion Mortar Mixing Plants - - - - - - -   39.27
       Insurance - 6% -   2.36

GC2 - Labor - Proportion General Organization Payroll - - - - 1,530.00
       Insurance - 1.75% - - - - - - - - - - - - - - - - - -   26.77

MT - Labor - Proportion Maintenance of Equipt- - - - - - - -   188.00
       Insurance - 8.516%- - - - - - - - - - - - - - - - - - -   16.01

              Patching - Gross Labor Cost - - - - - - - - - $76,194.93

Material

P-14 - Material - Brick,Tile,Lime,Sand, Cement, etc. - - - - - $ 5,801.49
GC14 -   "   - Proportion Hod Hoist Plant & Equipt- - - - -   846.06
GC14 -   "   -   "   Industrial Railway - - - - - - --   115.29
GC14 -   "   -   "   Mixing Plants - - - - - - - - -   66.43
MT -   "   -   "   Maintenance-Power-Water-Gas-Oil,etc   90.00

            Patching - Gross Material Cost - - - - - - - $ 6,919.27

)Tile - $33,245.68
Patching Gross Labor and Material Cost $83,114.20 (Brick- 49,868.52
                                        $83,114.20

The Average Gross Cost Per 1000 Bricks - Miscellaneous Patching - $4.50 M

  "   "   "   "   " Sq.Ft.Tile -   "   " - $.019

Net Labor Cost per 1000 Bricks - Miscellaneous Patching - $3.66 M

Net Labor Cost Per Sq. Ft. Tile   Patching - $.009 Sq.Ft.

Account	Description of Item		Amount	Cubic Feet	Unit Cost
	Brought Forward		$345,618.38	198,665	1.73674
8-D	<u>Cutting</u>	Labor	40,805.65	"	.20540
	(Includes Cutting for Lewis)	Insurance	3,511.73	"	.01768
	(and anchor holes, Trimming)	Material	--		--
	(etc.)				
8-E	<u>Cowing Compression Joints</u>	Labor	1,557.17	"	.00784
	8.606	Insurance	134.01	"	.00067
	(Includes Labor & Material)	Material	15,687.00	"	.07896
8-F	<u>Cleaning and Pointing</u>	Labor	15,507.53	"	.07896
	(Labor and Material) 8.606	Insurance	1,334.58	"	.00671
		Material	102.86	"	.00051
	Wm. Bradley & Son, Purchase Price of Stone		797,300.00	"	4.01320
	Sifter and De Cesare - Models		2,310.00	"	.01162
	Total,		1,223,868.91	198,665	6.16 per cu.ft.

Summary

Cost of Stone	4.0132	per cubic foot
Cost of Models	.0116	" " "
Cost of Cowing Lead Joints(Mat'l)	.0789	" " "
S.B.& Eken Labor	1.6565	" " "
" Insurance	.1353	" " "
" Plant (Mat'l.only)	.1550	" " "
" Material(includes)		
(scaffolds)	.1106	" " "
Gross Cost	6.16 per cubic foot	

Analysis, Starrett Brothers & Eken - Net Labor Cost

		Per Cu.Ft.
p l a n t	(Labor - Plant & Equip. Derrick & Hoist Erection,Dismantlg.etc..	.07122
	(" Proportion Material Hoist Equipment " " "	.03849
	(" Proportion Overhead Trolley System " " "	.00478
	(" Proportion Industrial Railway " " "	.00560
	(" Proportion Mortar Mixers " " "	.00131
	" Proportion of General Supt.Payroll	.10268
	" Setting	1.11862
	" Anchors	.00825
	" Mortar Mixing, etc.	.01338
	" Cutting	.20540
	" Cowing Compression Joints	.00784
	" Cleaning and Pointing	.07896
	Net Labor Cost	1.656

EMPIRE STATE BUILDING

Cost of Concrete Floor Arches to 85th Floor Inclusive

No Return Patching of Temporary Hoist
Openings Included

Account	Labor	Quantitied Placed	Unit	Amount
				$
SC9	Making -Hoisting,Placing Stripping			
	Forms for Beams and Girders	2,119,245 sq.ft.	$.1398	296,350.76
SC8	Making -Hoisting,Placing Stripping			
	Forms for Slabs or Decks	1,835,069 " "	.0593	108,901.48
SC25	Instlg. Beam and Girder Clips	649,253 Lin. "	.0174	11,290.42
SC19	Hdlg.& Instlg.Clip Chrs.on Pan.Bms.	--		1,168.57
SC18-A	Plcg.Wire Mesh Reinf.on Fl.Arches			
		2,691,242 sq.ft.	.0134	36,000.00
SC18-B	Plcg.Rod Reinf.for spandrel			
	Bms. & Incidental Fl.Panels			10,726.51
SC 1	Mixing & Plcg.Cinder Concrete	60,968 cu.yds	2.29	135,920.99
SC 4	Mixg. & Plcg. Stone Concrete	686 " "	3.38	2,321.91
GC14 Hoist	- Prop. Lab. on Matl.Hoist			
	Installation & Dismantling			14,339.35
GC14 Mixer	- Prop.Lab.on Concrete Plant			
	Installation & Dismantling			3,722.38
SCT	Maintenance			7,285.01
GC2	Proportion of Superv'sn.Payroll			23,800.00
GC4	Ins.Rate 1.75 on " Pyroll ($23,800.)			416.50
GC4	Ins. aver.rate 7.048 on Genl.Pyrolls($628,027.38)			44,263.37

Account	Material			
SC13	Lumber for all forms			37,162.85
SC25	Beam and Girder Clips			11,353.90
SC19	Chairs for Panel Beams			5,479.71
SC18-A	Wire Mesh Reinforcement			48,530.98
SC16 SC18-B	Rod Reinforcement			2,581.00
SC26	Haunch Stiffners and Wire Hangers			2,953.58
SC14	Nails - Spacers - Tie wire, etc.			20,917.16
SC1	Portland Cement - Sand - Cinders			262,947.88
SC4	" " " Crushed Stone			4,923.45
GC14 Hoist	- Proportion Hoist, Plant and Equipment			18,392.55
GC14 Conc.	" Concrete Equipment			5,843.26
SCT	Oil - Mtce. Power, Water			5,865.90

Completed Concrete Arch (excldg.return ptchg.) $1,123,459.47

2,791,000 sq.ft. $.4025

SC20 Hod - Miscl. Ptchg. of arches,screeding fire tower
       stairs,etc.   2,791,000 sq.ft. .0380   106,520.13

SC24 Return work on arches over temp.
       hoist opengs.   2,791,000 " "   .0309   86,235.58

108,183 sq.ft. $86,235.58 $792 per sq.ft.   1,316,215.18

Gross Cost .4716 sq.ft.

Net Labor Units on Concrete Arches

	Straight Time	Excess Time	Total	
SC8 Slab Forms	$.055	$.0043	$.0593	sq.ft.
SC9 Beam & Gird.Forms	.123	.0168	.1398	" "
SC25 Beam & " Clips	.015	.0024	.0174	lin ft.
SC18-A Wire Mesh Rnfct.	.012	.0014	.0134	sq.ft.
SC1 Cinder Concrete	2.05	.24	2.29	cu.yds.
SC4 Stone Concrete	2.93	.45	3.38	cu.yds.

Detailed Analysis of Cost of Erecting Limestone

Quantity   Set from Original Plans 198,328 cu.ft.
Add for Changes   337 " "
            Total Set in Place,   198,665 " "

Account	Description of Item	Amount	Cubic Feet	Unit Cost
GC14-Stone	Plant & Equipment Labor	$14,150.00	198,665	.07122
	(Derricks,etc.) 8.606 Insurance	1,217.77	"	.00612
	Material	18,562.58	"	.09343
GC14-Hoist	Proportion Hoist Equip. Labor	7,647.65	"	.03849
	8.606 Insurance	658.16	"	.00331
	Material	8,449.36	"	.04253
GC14-Overhead				
Trolley	Proportion O.H.Mono Rail Labor	950.00	"	.00478
	8.606 Insurance	81.76	"	.00041
	Material	2,627.25	"	.01322
GC14-Industrial				
Railway	Proportion Indus.Rwy. Labor	1,113.98	"	.00560
	8.606 Insurance	95.87	"	.00048
	Material	770.00	"	.00397
GC14-Mortar	Proportion Mortar Mix. Labor	261.85	"	.00131
Mixers	8.606 Insurance	22.53	"	.00011
	Material	367.90	"	.00185
GC2-Supervision	Labor	20,400.00	"	.10268
	Proportion of Supt. Payroll			
	1.75 Insurance	357.00	"	.00179
8-A	Setting Labor	222,231.14	"	1.11862
	(Includes Unldg.& Handling)			
	(Placing,Setting and) 8.606 Ins.	19,125.21	"	.09627
	(Erectg.& Scaffolding) Material	17,636.52	"	.08877
8-B	Anchors Labor	1,639.70	"	.00825
	(Includes Bending,Handlg. 8.606 Ins.	132.29	"	.00066
	(Dipping & Placing on Floor) Material	2,658.27	"	.01388
8-C	Mortar Labor	2,649.41	"	.01338
	(Includes Mixing,Handlg) 8.606 Ins.	228.00	"	.00114
	(& Placing Mortar) Material	1,584.18	"	.00797
	Carried Forward	345,618.38		1.73674

NOTES
ON
NOTES

The typescript manuscript *Notes on Construction of Empire State Building* documents the demolition of the late-nineteenth-century Waldorf-Astoria Hotel, located on the west side of Fifth Avenue between 33rd and 34th Streets in New York City, and the erection on the site of the Empire State Building. It contains seventy-seven numbered sheets of typed text (recto only) on standard notebook-size, blue-lined graph paper. Interspersed are thirty-two sheets of brown pressboard on which are mounted sixty-four black-and-white photographs ranging in size from 4.75 x 3.5 in. to 4.25 x 2.5 in. (12 x 9 cm./11 x 7 cm.), affixed by black corners. Each photograph is identified by a negative number, a date, and a brief caption, typed on white labels edged in red. There is a thirteen-page appendix of detailed figures of costs for materials, equipment, and labor. All these are collected in a commercially produced blue-gray cloth three-ring binder, 11.5 x 11 in. (30 x 28 cm.). The name "B.H. Richardson" is pasted on a label inside the front cover (Briton H. Richardson served as director and president of Starrett Brothers and Eken 1956–1957).

It is unclear if Richardson was responsible for the creation of the notebook, since its author or authors are uncredited. The document seems to have been compiled as an in-house project, perhaps in late 1930 and 1931. A clue to its dating, and maybe to its authorship, is an article published in *Architectural Forum* in April 1931 by John P. Carmody, who headed the Production and Costs Department of Starrett Brothers and Eken. Carmody's piece closely parallels the text of the notebook (which has a less polished writing style), and seems to be based on it. Ten additional articles on various aspects of the Empire State's construction were published in a series in *Architectural Forum* from January 1930 through May 1931 (see below); perhaps the different division

185

heads and subcontrators wrote sections on their respective areas, then someone strung them together in narrative.

Some of the notebook photographs appear in the *Architectural Forum* articles, as do many others that are not included in the notebook. The identifying negative numbers (into the 500s) suggest there were many more shots that have since been lost or perhaps were never printed. Such thorough documentation of the building process is unusual, though serial progress photographs commissioned by the builder have been a standard form of recording the work of large construction projects since the late nineteenth century. Usually they are taken every one or two weeks from the same camera position or multiple positions but they are always exterior views of the structure rather than of the work being performed. The 412 progress photographs of the Empire State—which had to be taken twice a week to record the rapid construction of the tower—are preserved in the Special Collections of Avery Fine Arts and Architectural Library at Columbia University in the City of New York. Also in Avery is another group of famous photographs of the building's construction, taken by Lewis Hine, who was commissioned by the public relations department of the Empire State and who focused his camera on the workers, both in action shots and in sensitive portraits.

Another fascinating record of the building's construction is a fifty-minute film, *Empires of Steel: A Story of a Supreme Achievement in Steel Construction*, produced by U. S. Steel in 1931. The movie traces the route of the steel from its fabrication in the Pennsylvania mill through its delivery and erection on Fifth Avenue. The film library of the Museum of Modern Art has a copy of this film.

Listed below are the articles on the design and construction of the Empire State published in *Architectural Forum* in 1930–1931:

Fred Brutschy, "The Empire State Building. VI. Plumbing," *Architectural Forum* 53 (1930): 645–646.

John P. Carmody, "The Empire State Building. X. Field Organization Methods," *Architectural Forum* 54 (1931): 495–506.

Irwin Clavan, "The Empire State Building: IX. The Mooring Mast," *Architectural Forum* 54 (1931): 229–234.

H. R. Dowswell, "The Empire State Building. XI. Materials and Construction," *Architectural Forum* 54 (1931): 625–632.

J. L. Edwards, "The Empire State Building. III. The Structural Frame," *Architectural Forum* 53 (1930): 241–246.

Bassett Jones, "The Empire State Building. VIII. Elevators," *Architectural Forum* 54 (1931): 95–100.

William F. Lamb, "The Empire State Building. VII. The General Design," *Architectural Forum* 54 (1931): 1–9.

Henry C. Meyer, Jr., "The Empire State Building. IV. Heating and Ventilating," *Architectural Forum* 53 (1930): 517–521.

H. F. Richardson, "The Empire State Building. V. Electrical Equipment," *Architectural Forum* 53 (1930): 639–643.

R. H. Shreve, "The Empire State Building. II. The Window-Spandrel-Wall Detail and its Relation to Building Progress," *Architectural Forum* 53 (1930): 99–104.

R. H. Shreve, "The Empire State Building Organization," *Architectural Forum* 52 (1930): 770–774.

Other useful sources include:

"The Empire State Building: New York City," *Architecture and Building* 54 (1931): 93–100.

Louis J. Horowitz and Boyden Sparkes, *The Towers of New York* (New York: Simon and Schuster, 1937).

Theodore James, Jr., *The Empire State Building* (New York: Harper and Row, 1975) 45.

Albert Kahn, "Designing Modern Office Buildings," *Architectural Forum* 52 (June 1930): 776.

"Paper Spires." *Fortune* (September 1930): 119, 122.

"Planning and Control Permit Erection of 85 Stories of Steel in Six Months," *Engineering News–Record* (August 21,1930): 281–284.

"The Skyline Builders," *Fortune* (December 1950): 95.

"Skyscrapers: Builders and Their Tools," *Fortune* (October 1930): 85.

Paul Starrett, *Changing the Skyline: An Autobiography* (New York: McGraw-Hill, 1938). The book was ghostwritten by Philip Freund.

W. A. Starrett, *Skyscrapers and the Men Who Build Them* (New York: Charles Scribner's Sons, 1928).

John Tauranac, *The Empire State Building: The Making of a Landmark* (New York: Scribner, 1995).

Carol Willis, *Form Follows Finance* (New York: Princeton Architectural Press, 1995).

——, "Form Follows Finance: The Empire State Building," in *The Landscape of Modernity*, Eds. David Ward and Olivier Zunz (New York: Russell Sage, 1992). 160–190.

INDEX

*(Page locators set in italic typeface
refer to text and illustrations
found in the reproduced
notebook.
The notebook pages are numbered
1 to 77 and commence after
text page 46.)*

A

American Bridge Company, 43
Architects, 18–20
Architectural Forum, Empire
    State series, 13, 27, 185–186
Asbestos Construction Co., *18*

B

Baker, Smith & Co., *18, 62*
Balcom, Homer G., 35, 36, 43,
    45
Bedrock, *facing 9, 9*
Bowser, J. W., 27
Brick/stonework, 28
  cost analysis, *following 77*
  curtain wall design, 36–37
  daily job activity log, *15–Δ188
16*
  dampproofing, *71*
  façade placement, *facing 35,
35*
  fireproofing of wall system, *facing 45*
  interior marble, *65–66*
  materials management, *facing
21, facing 23, facing 24, 25,
26, 32, 33*, 41
  quantities, *34*
  speed of construction, 28, 39
  tile and terrazzo, *facing 34, 34,
64*
Brown, Floyd, 15, 18
Builders. *See* General contrac-
    tors
Bungalows and shanties, *facing
11, facing 14, 11*

C

C. E. Halback & Co., *18, 47*
Campbell Metal Window Corp.,
    19, 68
Carmody, John P., 27, 185
Ceiling height, 20
Cement Finish Company, *19*
Changing the Skyline, 12, 13
Chrysler Building, 11, 13, 14,
    34, *42*
Cities Service Building, 13
Columns and beams
  basement, *facing 41*
  compression under load, 35,
    50
  design, 34–35
  fireproofing, *facing 41, facing
    44, 44*
  lower, design, *facing 42*
  pier, placement, *facing 43*
  weight, 11, 14
Concrete
  fireproofing, *facing 41, facing
    44*
  footings, *9*
  quantity, *facing 33*, 11, *34, 44*
Concrete floors
  construction process, *following
    43*
  cost analysis, *following 77*
  design, 35–36, *44*
  materials delivery, *facing 21,
    facing 32, facing 33, 25,
    33*, 41
  mesh, *following 43, 34, 35, 44*

speed of construction, 29, *41*
Contractors Glass Company, *20*
Cornerstone laying, *facing 76*
Cubical space, *51*
Curtain walls, 36–37
Cutler Mail Chute Company, *69*

D

Dahlstrom Metallic Door Co., *19*
Daily job activities, *14–20*
Dampproofing, *71*
David Lupton Sons Company, *68*
Demolition of Waldorf-Astoria Hotel,
   facing 5, 20, 40
  below grade, *facing 8*, 7
  debris, *1, 5, 6, 8*
  dust control, 7
  equipment and method, *6, 7, 8*
  façade removal, *facing 1*
  safety practices, *73*
  salvaged materials, *1, 2*
  souvenir seekers, *1*
  timeline, *5*
  workforce, *6, 8*
Depaoli, Del Turco Foscato
   Corporation, *64*
Depression, 29–30
Design/design process, 12
  curtain wall, 36–37
  decision to build, 14–17
  design team, 18–20, 22, 24, 36, 46
  economic blueprint, 17, 18
  electrical system, 37–38
  elevators/elevator service, *51–58*
  façade, 24, 36
  in fast-track construction, 45
  floor plans, 20–22
  height, 22–24
  interior marble, *66*
  plumbing, *61*
  predicted vs. actual height, 35
  site characteristics, 17, 18
  steel fabrication, 43
  structural elements, 34
  Waldorf-Astoria Hotel, *facing 4, 4*, 40
  zoning law, 17–18
Doors, *70*
du Pont, Pierre S., 14–15, 17
Dust control, 7

E

Economic height, 13–14
Eken, Andrew, 12. *See also* Starrett
  Brothers and Eken
Electrical system
  daily job activity, *17*
  design, 37–38
  hoist system signaling, 23, 24

installation, *59–60*
  transformers, *59*, 60
Elevators, 11, 14
  building design and, 22–24
  building height predictions, 35
  controls, 52
  daily job activity log, *16*
  design challenge, 51
  doors, 55, 58
  freight, *54*
  main passenger, *52*
  material hoists, *facing 36*
  night service, *52*
  safety in construction, 72–73
  scheduling, *54*
  shaft enclosure, *facing 34*
  signal system, *53*
  specifications, *56–57*
  Waldorf-Astoria Hotel, *3*
  worker transport, *facing 28, 28–31*,
   40, 42
Empire State Building
  construction milieu, 13–14
  decision to build, 14–17
  historical significance, 10, 11, 33,
   46, 77
Entrances, *facing 4866, facing 50*
Ev–Air-Tight Calking Co., *19*, 71
Excavation, *facing 9, 9*

F

Façade
  design, 24, 36–37, *45*
  exterior metal, 45, *46*, 47
  materials placement, *facing 35, fac-*
   ing 45, facing 46, facing 48, 35, 46,
   49, 50
  speed of construction, *41*
  Waldorf-Astoria Hotel, *facing 1*
Fast-track construction, 43–45
Fatalities, *74, 75, 76*
Financial management
  accounting department, *10*
  cost analyses, *following 77*
  daily labor unit cost, *10, 12*, 27–28
  estimated construction cost, 29
  final construction cost, 29
  general contractor's fee, 20, 27
  investor financing, 14–17
  labor cost distribution, *12*
  materials movement, *21*
  payroll system, *facing 12, 11, 12*, 27
  post-construction problems, 29–30
  projected operating costs, 18
Fire protection
  alarms, 37
  cementitious/concrete fireproofing,
   facing 41, facing 44, 44

  wall system, *facing 45*
  water system, *38, 39*
Floor plans, 20–22
Floors. *See* Concrete floors
Food services, *facing 13, 13*
Footings, *9*
Foundations
  cost analysis, *following 77*
  demolition of Waldorf-Astoria Hotel,
   facing 8, 7
  excavation, *facing 9, 9*
  grillage and piers, *facing 9, facing*
   43, 9
Frederic Hone & Co., *17*

G

General contractor
  in design process, 12
  responsibilities, 26–27
  selection, 20
  site offices, *facing 11, facing 14, 11*
  trends in construction management,
   39–40
  See also Starrett Brothers and Eken
George A. Fuller Company, 26
Grillage and piers, *facing 9, 9*

H

Harmon, Arthur Loomis, 20
Heating and ventilating
  daily job activity, *18*
  materials, *62*
Height, skyscraper
  determinants of, 22–24
  economic context, 13–14
  Empire State Building, 11, 14, 17,
   33–34, *42, 51*
  Manhattan 1920s, 13–14, 33–34, *42*
  predicted vs. actual, 35
  zoning envelope, 17–18
Hine, Lewis, 186
Hiring, *11*
Hoist system, *facing 21, facing 36,*
  21–24
Horowitz, Louis J., 12
HRH Construction, 9, 10
Hydro-Bar Corporation, *19, 70*

I

Innovation
  brick handling, *32, 33*
  fast-track construction, 46
  materials delivery, 28, 29, 40
Insurance, 72–73

J

J. C. McFarland Company, Inc., *70*
J. L. Murphy, Inc., *17, 61*

J. Livingston & Co., *17*
Jacob Ringle & Son, *18*
James Stewart and Company, 26
Job organization, 27
  chart, *facing 10*
  industry evolution, 39–40
  rationale, *10*
  unique features, 12
Job runners, *10*
Jones, Bassett, 22–24

K

Kaufman, Louis G., 15

L

L. K. Comstock & Co., *17*
L. S. Fischl's Sons, *20*
Labor
  cost analysis, *following 77*, *10*, 27–28
  cost distribution monitoring, *12*
  daily job activity log, *14–20*
  demolition of Waldorf-Astoria Hotel,
  6, 8
  fatalities, *74, 75, 76*
  food services for, *facing 13, 13*
  hiring, *11*
  job actions, 29
  payroll system, *facing 12, 11, 12*, 27
  safety and protection, 34, 72–75
  size/distribution of workforce, 12,
  14–20, 28
  steel frame, 38–39
  supervisory system, 27
  transport on site, *facing 28, 28–31,*
  40, 41–42
Lamb, William F., 20
Lewis, Horton, *facing 45*
Limestone, 28
  cost analysis, *following 77*
  cutting, *48*
  façade placement, *facing 35, facing*
  46, facing 48, 46, 48, 49, 50
  materials management, *facing 48,*
  facing 49, 29, 35, 41, 49
  origins, *48*
  piers, 36
  pressure relieving joint, *50*
  quantity, *35, 48*
Long Island Wire Works, *19*
Lovell, E. B., 35

M

Mail chutes, *69*
Manhattan Company Building (40
  Wall Street), 13, 14, 26, *42*
Marble, *65–66*
Marc Eidlitz and Son, 26
Martin Conroy & Sons, *20, 63*

Materials management
  brick handling, *32, 33*
  challenges, 38
  concrete, *facing 21, facing 32, facing*
  33, 25, 33, 41
  construction debris, *facing 27, 27*
  in demolition, 6, 40
  electrical transformers, *60*
  equipment, *21*
  exterior limestone, *facing 35, facing*
  48, facing 49, 35, 49
  exterior metal, 47
  hoist system, *facing 21, facing 36,*
  facing 40, 21–24
  innovation, 28, 29, 32, 40
  on-site, 40–41
  outside derricks, 26
  rail system, *facing 25, facing 26, fac-*
  ing 32, 25, 40, 41
  safety methods, *73–74*
  scheduling, 28, 41
  structural steel, 28, 38, 42–45
  for subcontractors, 36
  terra cotta tile, *facing 34, 34*
  to-site delivery, 41
  unloading, 32
McClintic-Marshall Company, 43
McCrom, Bill, *59*
Mechanical engineers, 22
Mechanical systems
  challenges, 37
  heating and ventilating, *18, 62*
  plumbing, *61*
  Waldorf-Astoria Hotel engine room, *3*
  See also Electrical system
Metal Door and Trim Co., *19, 70*
Meyer, Strong, and Jones, 22, 37
Mooring mast, *facing 76, 14, 35*
Movement of materials. *See* Materials
  management

N

Night watchman, 37
Notes on Construction of Empire State
  Building
  authorship, 9, 27, 185–186
  historical significance, 10, 33
  photographs and captions, 9–10, 186
  physical appearance, 9
  provenance, 9
  typescript, 185

O

Observation deck income, 14
Occupancy, 29–30
Office design, 20–22
Opening day, 29
Operating costs, original projections, 18

Otis Elevator Company, *17, 22*

P

Payroll system, *facing 12, 11, 12*, 27
Plastering, *63*
Plumbing
  design, *61*
  temporary water system, *38–39*
Post and McCord, Inc., *17*, 29, 43

R

Raskob, John Jacob, 15, 17
Real estate market
  cycles, 13
  economic height, 13–14
  Manhattan evolution, 15
  Manhattan 1920s, 13–14, 15–17
  Manhattan 1930s, 29–30
Richardson, Briton H., 185
Roofing, 67
Roosevelt, Franklin D., 29

S

Safety, 34
  during demolition, 73
  fatalities, *74, 75, 76*
  methods, *73–74*
  press reports, 75
  responsibility, 72
  supervisory personnel, 72–73
Scheduling. *See* Materials management
Sears Tower, 14
Security, *facing 14, 10*
  fire protection, 37, 38, *39*
  night watchman tour stations, 37
Setbacks, 17–18, 22
Shop drawings, 43
Shreve, Lamb, and Harmon, 18-20, 36
Shreve, Richmond M., 18, 22, 24
Silverman, Joel, 10
Site characteristics, 15, 17, 18
  bedrock, *facing 9, 9*
  history, *facing 9*
Skyscrapers and the Men Who Build
  Them, 12
Smith, Alfred E., *facing 76, 15*, 29, 75
Speed of construction
  impetus, 18
  influence on design, 36
  management for, 28–29
  projected vs. actual, *41*
  records, 29
  significance of Empire State Building, 11–12, 14, 33, 34, *40*, 46, 77
  skeletal frame, 38
  speed of demolition and, 40
  standards, 28, 39
  steel management, 43–45

structural determinants, 34, *41*
team design for, 24, 46
Square feet of rentable space
  Empire State Building, 11, 14
  office design, 20–22
  post-construction occupancy, 29–30
Starrett, Paul, 12, 13, 20, 22, 24, 26, 28, 29. *See also*
  Starrett Brothers and Eken
Starrett, William, 12, 26–27. *See also*
  Starrett Brothers
  and Eken
Starrett Brothers and Eken, 9, 10, 12, 20, 39
  demolition of Waldorf-Astoria, 40
  employees, 28
  history, 26
  pace of construction, 28–29
  responsibilities, 26–27
  supervisory system, 27–28
Steel frame
  beginning of erection, *facing 41*
  construction schedule, *42*
  erection, daily job activity log, *17*
  labor requirements, 38–39
  materials management, 28, 38, 42–45
  speed of construction, 28, 29, 34, 38, *41*
  suppliers, 43
  support for curtain wall, 36–37
  topped out, *facing 40, facing 76, 41*
  Waldorf-Astoria Hotel, *facing 1, facing 5, facing 7, 5, 6*

weight, 11, 14, *42*
See also Columns and beams
Subcontractors
  daily job activity log, *17-20*
  employees, 28
    exterior metal, *47*
  hiring of, 27
  materials management, *36*
  trends in construction management, 39–40
Supervision
  daily job activity log, *14*
  of labor cost distribution, *12*
  method, 27
  organizational structure, *10*
  safety methods/personnel, *72–73*
  timekeeping, *facing 14, 11*

T

Tenants, maximum, 14
Terrazzo, *64*
Thompson-Starrett, 12, 26
Tile, *facing 34, 34, 64*
  cost analysis, *following 77*
Todd and Brown, 26
Towers of New York, The, 12
Traitel Marble Company, 20, 65
Tuttle Roofing Company, 20, 67

U

United Engineers and Construction, 26

Waldorf-Astoria Hotel
  cantilever truss, *facing 6, facing 7*
  design, *facing 4, 4, 40*
  elevators, *facing 28, 3*
  engine room, *3*
  origins, 15
  steel frame, *facing 1, facing 5, 5*
  See also Demolition of Waldorf-Astoria Hotel
Walker, James J. (mayor), 29
Washington Concrete Corp., *19*
Water system, temporary, *38–39*
Weinfeld, Louis, 9, 10
William Bradley and Sons, 48, 66
William H. Jackson Co., *18, 47*
Windows, 11, 22
  dimensions, 20
  installation, *19*
  materials, *68*
Window-spandrel-wall system, 24
  caulking, *71*
  curtain wall design, 36–37
  design, *facing 45, 45–46*
  handling, *47*
  manufacturers/fabricators, *46*
  speed of construction, *41*
Woolworth Building, 33–34
World Trade Center, 14

Z

Zoning law, 17–18